HISTORIC TALES

— of —

WHOOP-UP COUNTRY

On the Trail from Montana's Fort Benton to Canada's Fort Macleod

Let's Whoop-it-up

Ken Robison

KEN ROBISON

THE
History
PRESS

Published by The History Press
Charleston, SC
www.historypress.com

Front cover: *A Hot Time in Fort Benton*, painted by Andy Thomas, depicts a true incident in Fort Benton in 1865 when a four-pound mountain howitzer strapped to the back of a mule was fired with surprising results while Native Americans looked on in amazement. *Courtesy of Andy Thomas*.

Back cover, bottom: Mule team on the Whoop-Up Trail on the way to Fort Whoop-Up. *Overholser Historical Research Center*; *inset*: Fort Whoop-Up, 2018. *Wikimedia Commons*.

First published 2020

Manufactured in the United States

ISBN 9781467146449

Library of Congress Control Number: 2020940196

Notice: The information in this book is true and complete to the best of our knowledge. It is offered without guarantee on the part of the author or The History Press. The author and The History Press disclaim all liability in connection with the use of this book.

To Montana's pioneers and indigenous peoples and our Canadian neighbors across the Medicine Line for our shared history and heritage.

To founder John G. Lepley and the Fort Benton River & Plains Society—past, present and future—for presenting history with verve.

To our Whoop-Up friends across the Medicine Line, Doren Degenstein, Gord Tolton, Mike Bruised Head and all:

"May the saddest day of your future be no worse than the happiest day of your past."

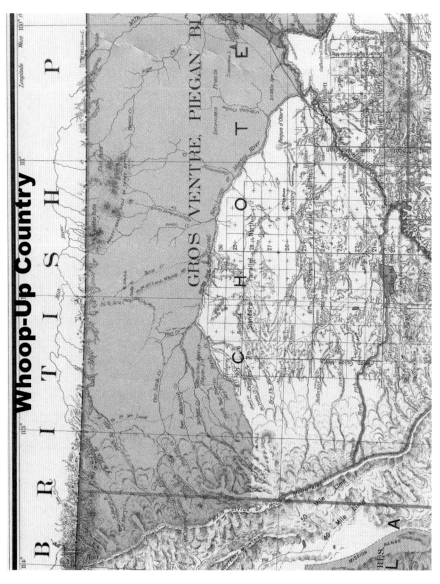

Whoop-Up Country from Fort Benton to the Rockies, from Sun River to the British Possessions. Montana Government Land Office Map, 1887. *Map reproduction courtesy of the Norman B. Leventhal Map & Education Center.*

CONTENTS

INTRODUCTION

Like spokes on a wagon wheel, trails and rivers radiate in every direction from the Birthplace of Montana. Leading from the west over the great falls to that birthplace, Fort Benton, flows the natural highway, the Missouri River, making this distant frontier town the world's innermost port and the commercial center for Montana Territory in the 1860s and '70s. Radiating out from Fort Benton were many trails: the Mullan Military Wagon Road, Northern Overland Trail, Cow Island Trail, Camp Cooke Trail, Graham Wagon Road and others. No trail was more important or notorious in its day than the Whoop-Up Trail, yet today this first international highway in the Northwest is largely forgotten. On this 150th anniversary, this is the story of the Whoop-Up Trail and Fort Whoop-Up and the prairie lands through which the trail passes, known as Whoop-Up Country. The Whoop-Up Trail extends from Fort Benton, northwest across the Medicine Line—the then unmarked and ill-defined international border—into western British America, today's Canadian provinces of Alberta and Saskatchewan. Fort Benton is the birthplace of Whoop-Up Country.[1]

The year 2020 marks the 150th anniversary of the birth of the fort, the trail and the country that bear the colorful name *Whoop-Up*. It all began in 1870 when the stage was set by the withdrawal of the Hudson Bay Company's monopoly from southwestern Canada the previous year. For fifteen years, from 1870 to 1885, trade goods, supplies, immigrants and adventurers came up the mighty Missouri River to Fort Benton by steamboat for transfer to overland freight wagons to follow a trail that assumed legendary fame and notoriety. Whoop-Up Country formed along the trail that passed through the broad, rolling prairie lands between Fort Benton, Montana Territory, northward across the Medicine Line into the newly formed Canadian North West Territory and westward to the Rocky Mountains.

WHOOP-UP TRAIL

Into the law-and-order vacuum left by the Hudson Bay Company, with no civil or military authorities and across an ill-defined border, in mid-January 1870, American traders John J. Healy and Alfred B. Hamilton commenced building a trading post, named Fort Hamilton, at the junction of the Belly and St. Mary Rivers (near today's Lethbridge) in the heart of Blackfoot Indian country. The post, soon known as Fort Whoop-Up, was the first and foremost of a chain of trading posts, often called "whisky forts," where Fort Benton free traders bartered a wide range of trade goods—rifles, ammunition, blankets, tobacco, sugar, knives, beads and whisky—with the Blackfoot and other Indian nations for bison robes, hides, furs and pelts. The trade goods were hauled in large Murphy wagons, by oxen or mules, along the two-hundred-mile trail from Fort Benton. For five years, from 1870 until 1875, this was a lucrative business, and the most skilled traders made small fortunes.

The riches to be made and the absence of law and order drew a wide mix of humanity, saints and sinners, leading to incidents and conflicts culminating in a battle in the Cypress Hills between Fort Benton traders and North Assiniboine (Nakota)—the "Cypress Hills Massacre." Responding to complaints from both sides of the border, the Canadian government in 1873 at last formed the North West Mounted Police (today's Royal Canadian Mounted Police) and sent them west the following year to establish law and order, close down the whisky trade and coerce the free traders back across the border into Montana. The result was lively and surprising.

With the arrival of the Mounted Police in the fall of 1874, Fort Benton merchants and traders realized that even more money could be made supplying the Mounted Police and encouraging the growth of frontier communities in what became the provinces of Alberta and Saskatchewan. So, as the Mounted Police closed down the whisky trading posts, the number of freight wagons on the Whoop-Up Trail from Fort Benton across the border actually increased. For the next decade, until the arrival of the Canadian Pacific Railroad in the prairie provinces in 1883, millions of dollars were made by Fort Benton merchant princes like I.G. Baker & Co. and T.C. Power & Bro. During these years, about one-third of the massive flow of cargo coming up the Missouri River to the Fort Benton levee was hauled by overland freight wagons over the Whoop-Up Trail to the newly formed Dominion of Canada.

In the post–Civil War era of the late 1860s, Fort Benton became home to a transient population, adventurers with wanderlust seeking opportunity. The frontier riverport boomed during steamboating season in the spring and summer with steamers arriving heavily loaded with passengers and freight, leaving mountains of cargo on the levee, and a massive overland freighting mix of wagons, oxen, mules and bullwhackers. Yet the town became nearly dormant during the winter. In those years, Fort Benton was a rough town with saloons and joints in the Bloodiest Block in the West operating day and night, a town of free-flowing whisky and quick triggers—so bloody that in 1869 the Blackfeet Indian Agency had to be removed ninety miles westward up the Teton River, near today's town of Choteau.

Fort Benton was a melting pot bordering on a powder keg. Many of these men had seen Civil War service, both North and South, and not a few had killed before. Many had Native wives, and it was well into the 1870s before the presence of White women became substantial. The remoteness and minimal law and order attracted many southerners, including Confederate soldiers and adventurous African Americans, many working on steamboats, and others trying out their freedom. They were joined by the Chinese who left the gold fields of southwestern Montana to operate restaurants, wash houses and opium dens. The Irish joined local southerners to keep Democrats in power politically throughout the new territory. Among the Irish in Fort Benton were an increasing number of Fenians, some coming directly from Fenian invasions of Canada, and all bringing their hatred for all things British. Beginning in 1869, a depleted U.S. Army infantry company was stationed in a newly formed Fort Benton Military District to provide a semblance of security.

Montana's indigenous tribes had grown increasingly dependent on trade and government annuities since the Lame Bull Treaty of 1855. These were the tribal lands of the Blackfoot Nation, the Nisitapi, composed of Siksika or Blackfoot; Kainai or Blood; Pikanii or Northern Peigan; and Pikuni or Southern Piegan. The Southern Piegan lived in northern Montana, while the other tribes were across the Medicine Line. The traditional lands of the

Blackfoot ranged from the North Saskatchewan to the Yellowstone River and from Cypress Hills, east of the Sweet Grass Hills, to the Rocky Mountains.[2]

A few notes are in order as the tales of Whoop-Up Country flow. Many of the stories and words come directly from the colorful pioneer participants in this saga—you will be reading, unfiltered, many stories of the Whoop-Up Trail, the trading posts, the colorful characters and the frontier times. These are real pioneers speaking in the words of their times—terms that may bother or offend today's reader: *savages, civilized, redskins, half-breed, bucks, squaws, papooses*. Let us understand their environment of culture clash and learn from these often tense, sometimes desperate times. Euro-Americans often appear as "Whites," while indigenous peoples are called Native Americans or Indian or even redskins. British/Canadian terms may differ from American spellings, such as Peigan and Blackfoot and whisky, north of the border, versus Piegan and Blackfeet and whiskey in the United States. For centuries, French fur traders married indigenous women, and their mixed offspring are referred to as Métis, while the offspring of Blackfoot and other indigenous women and American fur traders will be distinguished as métis. Since much of our story comes directly from those who lived in the times and "made" the history, remember this work is largely composed of their stories in their terms.

Canadian historians, led by the great Hugh A. Dempsey, have contributed most of the research and writing about the Whoop-Up era, its effects on the Canadian Blackfoot and the belated establishment of law and order with the coming of the Mounted Police. Their focus has been on whisky trading and its evil effects. Dempsey was critical also of the new Canadian government for its failure to establish law enforcement in Rupert's Land (the western prairies) and the Fort Benton "whisky traders," with particular blame placed on "exploiter par excellence" John J. Healy. Dempsey concluded that in just a few years, "a pattern emerged that made the Blackfoot easily susceptible to the siren songs of the Montana traders when they began to pour unlimited supplies of whisky into their camps in exchange for buffalo robes." The Canadian Blackfoot, according to Dempsey, "were swept into the maelstrom of alcohol, violence, and death." The conclusion easily reached by reading Canadian writing on the period is that nasty, low-life whiskey traders from Fort Benton invaded British America, seizing the wealth and women of Native Blackfoot at their whisky posts, devastating the prairie lands in a short period, most often stated as 1869–75.[3]

The times were often as brutally harsh as the Montana-Canadian weather, where forty-below-zero temperatures and blizzards were common. Yet both

Montanans and Canadians have tended to exaggerate for dramatic effect the traders, the whisky posts, the whooping-it-up environment. After all, neither the reconstructed Fort Whoop-Up near Lethbridge nor reconstructed Old Fort Benton Trading Post would be quite as exciting as tourist attractions and have quite their luster without the "whoop-up" stories, sometimes portrayed accurately, other times to the extreme. Similarly, most writing of the era emphasizes to the extreme Indian and Euro-American conflict, from minor skirmishes to major battles, as the cultures clashed. Yet continuing conflicts of historic enemies—such as Blackfoot-Cree and Blackfoot-Assiniboine— leading to horse capture raids, captive women, skirmishes, battles and even that glamorous word *massacres*, happened often, yet are little mentioned.

So, there is much to this complex story, and these complexities will be explored over the coming pages. As cultures clashed throughout the American and Canadian western lands, tension, culminating in violence, between Indians and Euro-Americans by no means began during the Whoop-Up era. Montana's first U.S. senator, Wilbur Fisk Sanders, believed that some two hundred White settlers were killed by Indians during the late 1860s and two thousand horses stolen. Incidents, including the burning of the Government Farm at Sun River and raids at Dearborn Crossing and along the Benton to Helena Road (the historic Mullan Road), became so commonplace that some settlers believed they were in an undeclared Blackfoot War. The frontier infantry—badly located first in 1866 at Camp Cooke, downriver from Fort Benton, and soon relocated in 1867 to Fort Shaw in the Sun River Valley, with a depleted company at Fort Benton—were simply too few in number to bring peace and order to this vast area, and most of these troops were infantry, without the mobility of cavalry.

Choteau County (later changed to Chouteau County in 1902), one of nine original counties in the new Montana Territory created in 1864, was vast, spreading from the Judith Basin to the Medicine Line and from the Rocky Mountains to the Little Rockies. The sheriff of that massive county and the several U.S. deputy marshals assigned to bring law and order on the Montana side could react in time to violence but could not prevent it.

Once the monopolies of the Hudson's Bay Company and the American Fur Company, and its 1865 successor North West Fur Company, were broken by the end of the 1860s, Fort Benton free traders, led by John J. Healy and Alfred B. Hamilton, moved across the border into the new North West Territory to establish trade more convenient for the tribes. The majority of their trade goods were essential items in demand among the Natives, including repeating rifles and ammunition. The Blackfoot and other

Indian Nations had long been groomed on alcohol, first by the Hudson's Bay Company and later by the American Fur Company. By 1870, the free traders of the Whoop-Up era found that the Natives, with few exceptions, would not trade without the inclusion of alcohol in the process. What Healy and Hamilton began as legitimate trade for robes within two years exploded into almost fifty unregulated and often competing fixed and mobile trading posts with hundreds of White traders, some Canadian, most Montanans, dispensing more and more alcohol among the Natives.

Since Whoop-Up Country became infamous in large measure for inclusion of whisky in the trade with indigenous peoples, Jim Hanson of the Museum of the Fur Trade emphasized: "It is important to note that consumption of alcohol was customary throughout society in America and the British possessions. Crews aboard fur trade boats expected to be supplied with alcohol while soldiers, sailors and many employees customarily received alcohol."[4]

As in the United States, the worst problem with liquor came after the Natives in Canada were forced onto reservations. Writing of the decade of 1885–95 on the Canadian plains, A.J. Haydon stated:

> Much illicit spirit was "run" into the country. It came in in every conceivable manner, in barrels of sugar, salt, and imitation eggs, in tins of tomatoes, in cases of boots, in ginger ale, and even in dummy bibles and prayer books. As it was possible for a saloon-keeper with a circle of friends who also held permits [government licenses given to White men to possess up to five gallons of liquor] to keep a good stock of liquor on his premises, the [North West Mounted] Police were often hoodwinked....Few Indians were proof against the wiles of the illicit whisky traders.[5]

Over the decades that followed, memories of the wild and wooly Whoop-Up era flowed forth in pioneer reminiscences and historical articles on both sides of the border. The "nasty, low-life whisky traders" emerged as exceptional frontiersmen like Howell Harris, Charles E. Conrad and Donald W. Davis settling the Canadian West. For every scoundrel, there were dozens of men of talent and ability. Scoundrels like Tom Hardwick were vastly outnumbered by future leaders of Montana, including seven later sheriffs of Choteau County.

Yet over the decades, memories of the Whoop-Up Trail and its era faded in the public mind. Small towns along the trail raised awareness on occasion

FORT BENTON-FORT MACLEOD TRAIL MARKER at Fort Benton

INSCRIPTION ON MARKER

The Fort Benton to Fort MacLeod or "Whoop-Up" trail into Canada was the main artery of commerce in the 1869-1883 era. Twenty yoke of oxen was a team and each team hauled three of the heavy freight wagons loaded with trade goods, calico and whiskey. They returned loaded with hides for the St. Louis market. Until the closing of the river trade this road was the source of supply for the Royal Canadian Mounted Police, the Boundary Survey and the Canadian Pacific Railway. The resourceful, fearless plainsmen and bullwhackers relaxed at the end of their hazardous journey, opened their cargo, not the calico, and "whooped it up." Thus the name "Fort Whoop-Up" and the famous "Whoop-Up Trail."

Placing of this marker in Old Fort Park was sponsored by Fort Benton M. I. A. history group

The trail leading from Fort Benton to Fort Whoop-Up in the lawless period of the early 1870s became known as the Whoop-Up Trail. *Author's photo.*

by promoting stories or events, and one Montana town even holds an annual "Whoop-Up Trail Days" celebration. Both Lethbridge and Fort Benton have held joint celebrations for dedication of a trail marker or a Whoop-Up Historical Pageant. While the memories have faded, the shared bonds remain to this day.

Bonds with Canada and memories of the Whoop-Up Trail rose during August 2005, when fifteen members of the River & Plains Society, keepers of Fort Benton's museums and history, traveled north along the Whoop-Up Trail, along modern highways, across a now well-defined and marked Medicine Line to the Lethbridge area to visit and tour reconstructed Fort Whoop-Up. The Fort Benton group, symbolically representing free traders and led by Executive Director John G. Lepley, was hosted at a breakfast and given a special tour by Fort Whoop-Up director Doran Degenstein and historian Gord Tolton.

Proceeding on to Fort Macleod, the Fort Benton group participated in the official opening of the historic North West Mounted Police Barracks at Fort Macleod, where 131 years earlier, in the fall of 1874, the first contingent of Mounted Police arrived to establish law and order and shut down Fort Whoop-Up and the other whisky posts north of the border. The Mounted Police built their headquarters at Fort Macleod, named for their

John G. Lepley (*left*) and Bob Doerk (*right*) of the River & Plains Society inspecting an original 1832 cannon taken by Johnny Healy from Fort Benton to Fort Whoop-Up in 1869. *Author's photo.*

Reconstructed Fort Whoop-Up display with interpretive sign for the Whoop-Up Trail. *Author's photo.*

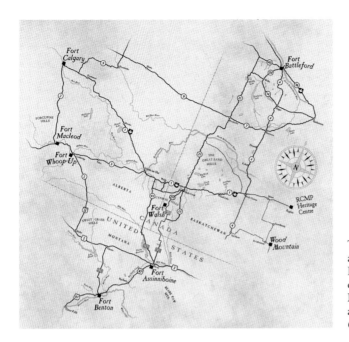

The Old Forts Trail, an International Historic Trail combining forts in Montana, Alberta and Saskatchewan. *OldFortsTrail.com.*

commander, Colonel James F. Macleod. One decade later, a large barracks complex was constructed at Fort Macleod; it was used until the 1930s, when it was dismantled. In 2003, a Canadian preservation group, the Riders of the Plains, began to reconstruct the huge complex, with an eventual goal of some fifty buildings. On August 25, 2005, the official opening of the North West Mounted Police Barracks (reconstructed) was held at Fort Macleod, with dignitaries from Ottawa and Calgary and their Fort Benton guests. Sharalee Smith of Fort Benton announced the addition of Forts Whoop-Up and Macleod to the Old Forts Trail. The Fort Benton delegation were guests at the dedication ceremonies and a banquet that followed, with a splendid performance of the Royal Canadian Mounted Police Musical Ride led by Commissioner Giuliano Zaccardelli.[6]

The Whoop-Up story is far more than a tale of trade and trading; it is the story of clashing cultures, strong and colorful men and women, Native, Euro-American and African American, overcoming harsh conditions and experiencing adventures galore. Whoop-Up Country saw tribal clashes between ancient ancestral enemies, tensions leading to conflicts between Natives and White and Black settlers and traders. In the 150 years since Fort Whoop-Up and the other trading posts began operations north of the border, triggering the formation of the North West Mounted Police and leading to the settlement of the prairie provinces, Fort Benton and western Canada have shared a strong historic bond. That bond is today alive and well in Whoop-Up Country on both sides of our international border of friendship. Today, the Whoop-Up Trail is largely forgotten, yet its history, and the many legends of Whoop-Up Country, are celebrated in communities on both sides of the border. *Historic Tales of Whoop-Up Country* will bring Fort Whoop-Up, the Whoop-Up Trail and the legendary characters back to life.

1

THE WILD TIMES

FORT BENTON AND THE FREE TRADERS

In Montana Territory, the placer mines were playing out by the end of the 1860s, incidents between Native Indians and Euro-American settlers were increasing, intertribal warfare continued and smallpox was ravishing the Blackfoot tribes; north of the Medicine Line, the Hudson's Bay Company's monopoly over vast western British America was ending—what would happen next in this far-distant land, this powder keg, that would become Whoop-Up Country?

The beauty of the Upper Missouri region inspired all who traveled through its rugged grandeur. Dramatic events during the 1860s transformed the region from the isolation of the fur and bison robe trade to the raucous gold rush days that would keep the region in turmoil throughout the Civil War and after. From the presence of thousands of Native Americans with several hundred White Americans clustered at several trading posts in 1860 to more than seventeen thousand miners and adventurers stampeding from gold strike to strike among the mining camps, the Upper Missouri region that became Montana Territory in 1864 was in turmoil during the Civil War years. The newly formed territory and its mining camps became exiles of choice for many southern soldiers and families as well as adventurers from the North. This was a transformational moment on the Upper Missouri in the heart of Native Blackfoot country.[7]

Fort Benton, the world's innermost port at the head of steamboat navigation on the Missouri River, transformed from a remote fur and robe trading post into the heart of a growing commercial empire that, within

American Fur Company Fort Benton Trading Post in August 1860. Photo by Lieutenant James Hutton. *Overholser Historical Research Center.*

a decade, would extend from the Dakotas to the Idaho mines and from Wyoming northward into British America, later comprising Alberta and Saskatchewan provinces.

Massive cargoes of freight and numbers of travelers arriving by steamboats bound for the gold fields of the new El Dorado transformed Fort Benton and the region. Still distant from the States, Fort Benton was no longer simply an extension of St. Louis as a trading outpost but rapidly emerging as the center for a commercial empire.

This all began in the summer of 1860. Until then, Fort Benton and nearby opposition post Fort Campbell were the focus of White American activity on the Upper Missouri River, together with Fort Owen and a few other settlements west of the continental divide. During that summer of 1860, three events occurred that set the stage for change. The first steamboats arrived at the Fort Benton levee from St. Louis with the first U.S. military unit, Major George A.H. Blake's three hundred troopers of the First Dragoons onboard; the William F. Raynolds Expedition arrived after exploration of the Yellowstone and Missouri Rivers and First Lieutenant John Mullan arrived with his joint military-civilian road-building expedition, completing the 624-mile Military Wagon Road from Fort Walla Walla, Washington Territory, to Fort Benton. The Blackfoot Indians, long dominant in the vast region, were about to be shaken from their isolation from White encroachment. Steamboats from St. Louis to Fort Benton and a wagon road to the Pacific set the stage for change in the region.[8]

Three decades earlier, fur trading posts with the Blackfoot (or Nitsitapi) and Gros Ventre (or A'aninin) reached the Upper Missouri. In that year,

Gustav Sohon painted this scene of the first arrival of steamboats at the Fort Benton levee in 1860. Lithograph by Bowen & Company. *Author's collection.*

the American Fur Company (after 1834 formally known as the Upper Missouri Outfit of Pierre Chouteau Jr. & Co. of St. Louis) opened a series of posts, first Fort Piegan (1831), followed by Forts McKenzie (1832), Chardon (1844), Lewis (1845) and Benton (1846–47). In 1846, an opposition trading post, Fort Campbell, financially supported by St. Louis trader Robert Campbell, was established two miles upriver from Fort Benton. Mackinaws and keelboats laboriously brought upriver from Fort Union at the Dakota border served as transportation before steamboats, bringing trade goods up and taking furs and bison robes downriver. The trading posts were more than businesses; they also served as conduits for news and ideas and as centers for exchange of customs and culture between Native Indians and the traders.[9]

North of the Medicine Line in British America, in Rupert's Land, the Hudson's Bay Company (HBC) merged with the North West Company in 1821, ending their fierce competition. For the decades before the first competition with Americans on the Upper Missouri at Fort Piegan, the HBC was the source of tobacco, blankets, knives, iron arrow points—and alcohol. For many years, the British provided brandy or rum as a key part of their trade with the Natives. The Blackfoot and other neighboring tribes acquired the taste—in essence were groomed—for alcohol long before Fort

This painting by David Parchen of Fort Campbell depicts the opposition trading post on the upper levee at Fort Benton. *Author's collection.*

Piegan opened for business in 1831. Fort Benton historian Joel Overholser captured the setting well:

> One fact became apparent, the tribesmen had no reason to learn to fancy whisky. They had already acquired the taste before [James] Kipp keyed his grand opening of Fort Piegan on the conversion of a barrel of alcohol into a three-day wingding. Two years later at Fort McKenzie, [Prince] Maximilian [of Wied] repeatedly commented on the thirst of Indian visitors. The source of the taste was unquestionable. In fact, David Mitchell of [Fort] McKenzie implied in a long talk with Maximilian that American Fur would be content to drop the trade in intoxicants as he claimed the company had in the Mandan area. But he noted that the fort's customers would trade at HBC forts if the Americans offered no whisky.[10]

Alcohol was the subject of Canadian historian Hugh Dempsey's book *Firewater*, and he wrote about this "liquid death" in terms as strong as ever used by the Woman's Christian Temperance Union:

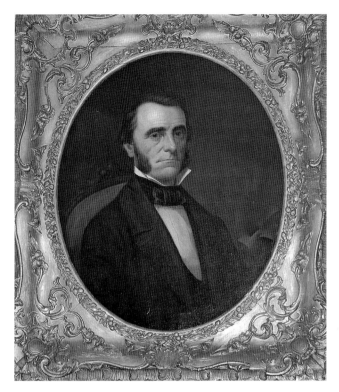

Alexander Culbertson, founder of the American Fur Company's Trading Post at Fort Benton, painted by John Mix Stanley in 1856. Displayed at the Dean & Donna Strand Gallery, Fort Benton. *Author's photo.*

Rupert's Land, composed of the Hudson's Bay drainage, was held under charter by the Hudson's Bay Company until 1869. *Wikimedia Commons.*

The whisky-trading era was relatively brief, about six years, but its effects were more devastating than any epidemic or massacre. Not only did the trade kill many people, but for the Blackfoot tribes, it devastated their cultural and social life, created internal dissension, and left them helpless in the face of the invasion of their hunting grounds by enemy tribes. Chiefs lost their power to control their bands, fathers could not control their young men and the rush to sell their robes and everything they owned for whisky turned many families into virtual paupers....

They [the Blackfoot] did not deserve to be decimated, victimized, and pauperized by the illicit trade in a deadly commodity that was foreign to their culture.[11]

Clearly, the Natives wanted the goods, and whisky, offered on both sides of the ill-defined boundary, and thus they tolerated Whites in their trading posts. Remarkable James Willard Schultz, who lived with the Blackfeet after 1870, wrote about "the company": "They sold watered rum and scotch whisky. We sold watered American alcohol and whiskey. I claim that we were just as respectable as the honourable lords and members of the Hudson's Bay Company, Limited."[12]

American and British traders accepted a "truce" over several decades. Yet all was not well for the HBC as the trade shifted from furs to the much heavier bison robes. The HBC had a long river and portage route that limited the number of robes that the canoe-based transportation system could handle. Meanwhile, as steamboat technology advanced, the mighty Missouri River became a natural highway for steamboats, first to Fort Union, at the confluence of the Yellowstone River, with large keelboats laboriously completing the trip to the Upper Missouri. Finally, by 1860, steamboats were landing at the Fort Benton levee, completing the natural highway to the head of navigation.

During the 1860s, few Americans ventured north into HBC country—the gold discoveries from 1862 to 1866 kept most adventurers stampeding from camp to camp in southwestern Montana Territory. Jesuit missionary Father DeSmet ventured as far north as the HBC post at Fort Edmonton in 1845. During the Montana gold rush, several incursions north of the border came, including adventures by both Americans and British Canadians in 1864, described by a descendant of Canadian Sam Livingston:

In 1864, Sam [Livingston] went north prospecting for gold in the Kootenai area, and while in Wild Horse creek met James Gibbons, a pioneer of the Edmonton area. Many other prospectors were there at this time and word came in from Edmonton that a fine type of gold had been found on the North Saskatchewan. Most of the prospectors did not know how to handle this type of gold, however, Sam said that he had found the same kind of gold on the Pend d'Oreille and knew how to save it. With Sam's assurance of his help a party of the prospectors decided to head for the North Saskatchewan.

The north bound group consisted of James Gibbons, Sam Livingstone, Johnny Healy, Charley Thomas, Joe Kipp, a man called Big Tex [Cass Huff] and others, almost fifteen in all. They came up through the Kicking Horse Pass to Banff and are said to have washed their shirts in the Bow River just below the present Canadian Pacific Railroad (C.P.R.) Hotel. From here they tried a cross-country route, from Banff to Rocky Mountain House, but as there was no trail and travelling was too difficult they returned to Banff and followed the Bow River east to open country. Here they had a disagreement; some thought the Bow was the Saskatchewan, so they split into three parties, one going south to Montana, one working on the Bow and the other, consisting of Sam Livingston, Tom Smith, James Gibbons and Big Tex going north toward Rocky Mountain House.

They had started out with lots of provisions and ammunition, but drifting about looking for the trail, lost time, used up their provisions, and by amusing themselves with seeing who could shoot off the greatest number of heads of fool hens (prairie chickens) they soon found themselves scarce of ammunition. By October, they had to turn to eating their own horses, and for a month mainly subsisted upon these. "Pretty hard living," was Mr. Gibbons' only comment. A party of Blackfeet stole what horses they had left, and the men, after caching their bedding set out on foot through the bush.

They followed a travois trail on the snow with no knowledge of where it led and at last, more dead than alive, weak with hunger, they reached Rocky Mountain House. Within the fort, Chief Factor [Richard] Hardisty gave the miners a hearty welcome, and gave them the best he had, rabbit stew. After a week's rest at [Rocky] Mountain House, the party pushed on to Edmonton on snowshoes, eating rabbit stew for food again.

Adventurous
Indian trader
John J. Healy.
*Overholser Historical
Research Center.*

It was December 1864, when they reached Fort Edmonton, then in charge of Chief Factor Christie. [They were turned away so went seventy miles down the Saskatchewan River to the Methodist Mission under Reverend George McDougall. Wintered there. Mined in the spring for gold.][13]

MEET ADVENTUROUS JOHN J. HEALY

With his group of prospectors, Sam Livingston mentioned a colorful American adventurer, John J. Healy, who came west with army dragoons and discovered gold at Florence, Idaho Territory. After prospecting in British America in 1864, Healy operated a trading post at Sun River Crossing with his brother Joseph, and in 1870, with partner A.B. Hamilton, Healy moved across the Medicine Line into the new North West Territory to open Fort Hamilton trading post. John J. Healy became the most prominent player in Whoop-Up Country. He later wrote a series of articles, published by this author in *Life and Death on the Upper Missouri: The Frontier Sketches of Johnny Healy*, about his years as a free trader on the Upper Missouri. He wrote briefly about his gold prospecting expedition in 1864 into British America in a very different tone than that of Sam Livingston.

Bucking the Hudson Bay Company

The term "Free Trader" has an easy, go-as-you-please swing; but in the old pioneer days of the sixties and earlier it carried a meaning that can hardly be understood in these peaceful times. It meant war—and war to the knife! The man who started out to buck any of the big trading companies went against the stiffest kind of warfare that was to be found in the whole wilderness.

The stories of the men who went down would furnish the darkest page in all the pioneer history of the Northwest. Of course, all this has changed: but there are some experiences in the fights waged by "free" trappers and traders that stick in the memory of the men who went through them. I confess that, for one, I haven't forgotten the struggles of this sort, and I believe they should be given a place in history of the old trading days. One of the toughest trips I ever made was in bucking the Hudson Bay Company, for it amounted to that before I wound up the experience.

That was in 1862 [*sic*, 1864], and I was then only twenty-three years old and had plenty to learn. Like all the traders and trappers in the Northwest States I listened to the tales of gold brought down by the Indians from the Dominion, and they tickled my ears. However, I was not the only white man whose head was turned by these rumors of how the Indians traded a gun barrel

Flag of the
Hudson's Bay
Company.
*Wikimedia
Commons.*

full of gold dust for a gun barrel full of powder. So, I determined to cross the line and look for gold in the Fort Edmonton country.

Luck seemed to be on my side at the outset of the undertaking. There was no excitement on the trip north, and when I struck the district where I intended to prospect. I stumbled on Brazos and Flet [Brazeau and Flett], two good men I had known on the Missouri. They came from Carondelet, the French settlement just below St. Louis. Brazos had been with the American Fur Company, but the Hudson Bay folks had induced him to bring his trade over to them about thirteen years before. Brazos gave me the best he had, and also told me the things I wished to know about the country.

"If you send any of your men up here," said he, "have them bring what they'll need in the way of food." That was as straight a hint as anyone would need from the trader of a Hudson Bay post! But I thought I could make a rich strike in gold, and so made my plans to go back and send up some of the men who were sure to be with me in any venture I should tackle.

"I'll not cross that hostile Blackfoot country," I told Brazos, "without rigging up to stand off the stiffest kind of an attack, and I'll come in condition to stick it out."

Then I started back to Fort Benton with a young half-breed Blackfoot as my only companion.[14]

FORT BENTON: FROM REMOTE TRADING POST TO RAUCOUS COMMERCIAL CENTER

In less than a decade, Fort Benton, the head of navigation on the Missouri River, boomed. It emerged from the American Fur Company trading post that in 1860 consisted of only the trading post with no town. Civilian John Strachan, with John Mullan's Roadbuilding Expedition, described the environment in the summer of 1860 in a letter written to his brother for publication in the *Rockford (IL) Register*:

> Fort Benton at last appeared in sight, and the prospects for home now began to brighten. Although yet distant over three thousand miles from St. Louis, the river from here is navigable, and we could now see the prospects of an outlet from this desolate region. Fort Benton belongs to the American Fur Company, is upon an extensive scale, and is worthy of the vast interest of which it is the center. Everything may be had within the Fort. They have a bakery, blacksmiths', carpenters' and coopers' shops; trade offices for buying, others for selling, for keeping accounts, and for transacting business; and also shops for retail. Goods are sold at enormous prices, the stock consisting of cotton and woolen goods, ready-made clothing, ship chandlery, tin and iron ware, fancy articles, and, in short, everything of every kind and description, including all sorts of groceries. Sugar is sold at one dollar and upward per pound, and everything else in proportion. The business here amounts to about $160,000 a year [$5 million today]; buffalo robes the staple of the trade. All is arranged in the best order, and I should think, with great economy.[15]

In 1860, Fort Benton served also as the outfitting post for the slowly growing colony of White Americans in Bitter Root, Deer Lodge and Missoula outposts. The first year of the Civil War brought little change on the upper river, yet as 1862 dawned, dramatic change was coming. That year brought placer gold strikes first at Gold Creek, north of Deer Lodge, then on Grasshopper Creek, causing the sudden formation of the mining camp of Bannack. The influences of the Civil War began to affect the Upper Missouri with the arrival of the first influx of those who had been in the war, either as participants or as observers. Many of the early arrivals came from Missouri, and the pattern quickly formed for the Upper Missouri to become the exile of choice for those who sought to avoid war or had briefly participated, only to become disillusioned by defeat or paroled after capture. Many of these, in the early years of the war, were Southern-sympathizing Missourians.

By the mid-1860s, the frontier town of Fort Benton grew rapidly during the spring and summer steamboating season with hundreds of freighters present to participate in large-scale overland freighting. By 1867, miners, freighters and steamboat passengers were greeted by a daunting array of saloons, dance halls and brothels centered on one block of Front Street facing the steamboat levee. This "Bloodiest Block in the West" roared twenty-four hours a day, and everything was legal.

From early spring until late fall, gambling houses with no betting limits pried the gold dust from miners. Faro, blackjack, poker and craps relieved many miners of their summer earnings before they returned to the States. Whisky captured its share, and fancy ladies finished off what was left of a miner's poke before he boarded the boat to St. Louis. The most infamous proprietor was Eleanor Dumont, known as Madame Moustache. She packed two revolvers and forced a steamboat carrying smallpox from the levee. Dumont's Cosmopolitan was one of the most popular saloons. There, Madame Moustache played blackjack at a raised corner table and served booze and girls to all takers.

Other infamous institutions along the Bloodiest Block in the West were Dena Murray's Jungle, Mose Solomon's Medicine Lodge, Break-of-Day Saloon, Squaw Dance and Board of Trade. In the words of William Gladstone, a visitor from British America:

> One could never tell when Sunday came around as there was no distinction made between that day and any other. Drinking and gambling and whiskey-selling went on just the same. On my first Sunday there I went to hunt up some friends and opening the door of the room where they lived, found four eager-eyed gamblers hard at work.
>
> Each man had a bag of gold dust and a pistol on the table before him. One of the men asked me if I was one of the parties that had just arrived from the north. I said, "Yes" and he asked me about the mines.
>
> "Stranger, do you indulge?" he hospitably asked upon my admitting that now and again on rare occasions, I was known to do so, he pointed to a bucket and told me that I would find some knock-me-down in there.

Model of Fort Benton's Bloodiest Block in the West in 1867, open twenty-four hours a day, where anything was legal and infamous Madame Moustache operated the Cosmopolitan Saloon, while Mose Solomon ran the Medicine Lodge. *Author's photo.*

> I dipped some of the liquid fire out of the bucket and asking for water was directed to another bucket which I found contained whiskey too. They all laughed at me and asked if they drank water where I came from as water in Benton was never used for that purpose.
>
> Oh, those were great days in Benton! Shooting and stabbing and rows of all kinds were daily occurrences and it was a wonder to me that more men were not killed.[16]

The racial environment in Fort Benton was complex. In 1862, four free Black men worked for the American Fur Company. As the town of Fort Benton developed, increasing numbers of Black settlers began to arrive on steamboats, often as crewmen, sometimes as passengers. Others came overland on emerging transportation routes. By 1870, Fort Benton's Black community had at least twenty-five citizens, and the growth of both the town and its Black community was accelerating. A decade later, some seventy-six Black residents were present in Fort Benton, and both the newly formed Choteau County and Fort Benton showed the highest percentage of Black occupancy of any county or city in Montana Territory. The town had a tradition of mixed race and nationality, with general acceptance of fur trader intermarriage with Native American women. Many of the early fur traders were of French or Canadian descent, and most early residents came upriver from St. Louis. Fort Benton became known as an extension of that gateway to the West.

Early Fort Benton featured a multiracial melting pot: Euro-Americans, mixed-race children of White/Black descent and White/Indian, Black Americans, Chinese and Native Indians. Among the Whites, too, there was a diverse mix of the old resident fur traders and a new influx from the border states and immigrant Irish. An important final element in early Fort Benton was the presence of a U.S. Army infantry company from a regiment stationed nearby at Fort Shaw. From 1869 to 1881, army officers, some with wives, and soldiers were present, influencing security and social affairs.

The many Native wives of White men formed a special category, numerous and accepted for many years until large numbers of White women began to arrive by the late 1870s. Many families in Fort Benton in the 1860s and 1870s involved interracial marriages of Indians and Whites and at least four White and Black marriages. Among the 523 residents of Fort Benton in 1878 were 34 Native wives, with 93 mixed-race White-Native children as well as 31 White-Native adults. At that time, about 34 percent of Fort Benton's population was non-White or mixed race.[17]

Piegan Blackfeet family. *Author's collection.*

LEAN, BLOODY YEARS AHEAD

In May 1869, the Union Pacific Railroad became the nation's first transcontinental railroad, bringing cargo by rail to Utah and greatly stimulating overland freighting north to Montana Territory in competition with steamboats. The placer gold mines were playing out, and that was a bloody year along the Benton to Helena road from Native raids and attacks. Montana's population surge was leveling off, with just twenty thousand Montanans counted in the 1870 census. The American Fur Company had sold out to the weaker North West Fur Company in 1865, opening cracks in the door for free traders such as John J. Healy to begin robe trading at Sun River Crossing.

North of the border in 1869, the Hudson's Bay Company's two-hundred-year-long charter for Rupert's Land over almost half the future nation of Canada ended, with the company paid a bargain price of £300,000 for its vast landholdings. Suddenly, there was no longer legal authority or potential law enforcement in the vast newly formed North West Territories. The new Dominion of Canada had no ability to impose authority on what became its own wild west, without settlements or settlers, and without law and order.

A useful reminder of the past glory of the Hudson's Bay Company appeared in the *Helena Independent* at the time:

Hudson's Bay Company

> The following in relation to the Hudson's Bay Company, which is now a story of the past, the company having transferred all its rights and property to the Dominion Government—will be of interest to the general reader.
>
> The Hudson's Bay Company is a name, which sounds of rich, warm furs, of victorine and muff, cuffs and gloves, caps, hats and coats—warmth brought from the frigid North, to adorn and warm more Southern beauty. It is the oldest regular stock company of the world. Its stock has rained fortunes. While its authoritative powers have been bartered away, its showers of gold will fall none the less copiously for those fortunate English and Scotch families, who pass its limited stock from generation to generation with a uniformity akin to the heraldic titles of the nobility. The company was organized 206 years ago. It obtained a charter from Charles II., in 1670. Its first dividend was made

over two centuries ago—December, 1673. By virtue of the charter the company was allowed the exclusive privilege of establishing trading factories on Hudson's Bay and its tributary rivers. They had comparatively insignificant rivalry for more than a century. A new charter, granted in 1821, gave exclusive license of trade for twenty-one years, from May 30, 1838, in all the northwestern British territory not included in their original charter, and placed them in possession of all....

This territory...is immense, and has given multitudes of men employment. The company has its governor-general, headquarters at York Factory, on the west shore of Hudson's Bay. Its clerks were generally young Scotchmen, who allied with them females of the natives, thus creating the present race of the Northwest—the "dear half-breeds" of Monsignor Fache, Bishop of St. Boniface, author of several works on the Northwestern territory, a warm friend of Riel, the murderer of poor Scott, of Toronto, Ontario, and but a few months since elected to the Dominion Parliament by acclamation—having no opposition at the hustings. There was no great radical change in the trading privileges after the expiration of the exclusive lease in 1869. It has retained the bulk of trade, although all the work is free to come and hunt and deal in furs. Its ruling influence is still felt, however. This is because of its wealth, its perfect organization, and superior knowledge of the country and its people.[18]

Just to the east, in Manitoba, during 1870 and 1871, several thousand Métis—mixed French and Native Cree and Chippewa—led by visionary Louis Riel, rose in rebellion to maintain their rights to land. Supported by members of the American Irish Fenian Brotherhood, the rebellion established a provisional government but was met by military force from Ottawa. Louis Riel was sent into exile in Montana, while Fenians like Civil War Union veteran "General" John J. Donnelly moved on to join the growing Irish and Fenian residents of Fort Benton. The Fenian goal to seize and occupy Canada to exchange for a free Irish Republic would remain a gleam in the eye of many Irishmen.

The door across the Medicine Line was ajar, and the stage was set in Fort Benton for free traders to look toward the north into the lawless North West Territory. Many factors were at play in the late 1860s in Fort Benton. The general postwar mix of Yankee and Rebel veterans of that defining moment

THE TRIAL AT REGINA, N.W. TERRITORY, OF LOUIS RIEL, THE LEADER OF THE RECENT HALF-BREED REVOLT IN CANADA

Visionary Métis leader Louis Riel on trial for leading the 1885 rebellion in the Red River Valley. *Author's collection.*

in American history were present in large numbers. All were trained soldiers, many bearing the scars of wounds and others the mental scars from the battlefield. This was a period of tension between Republican administrations in Washington, D.C., and their federal officers in Montana versus dominant Southern Democrats and their Irish Democrat allies in Montana Territory, controlling the territorial legislature. The was increasing tension between Natives and White settlers—raids and horse stealing from 1865 on with the environment in Fort Benton so explosive that the Blackfeet Indian Agency had to be removed and relocated in 1869 to the upper Teton (near today's town of Choteau). Notably, both Montana and Fort Benton had growing Irish populations—and the Irish, whether Fenians or not, had a hatred of the British for their invasion and occupation of Ireland. Many of these Irish were men of uncommon ability and talent, like John J. Donnelly, army veteran and future Speaker of the Montana House of Representatives; John Tattan, army veteran and longtime judge; John H. Evans, army veteran and natural leader of men in war and peace; and John J. Healy, an army veteran whose achievements and setbacks became legend. All these complex

John J. Healy's trading post at Sun River Crossing is partially imbedded in this modern home. *Author's photo.*

factors came into play in Fort Benton during the late 1860s—and became important in the years that followed.

Meanwhile, about fifty miles west of Fort Benton, on the Benton to Helena Road, free trader John J. Healy was setting the stage for his move northward from his trading post at Sun River Crossing. Healy wrote of recent intertribal warfare, an attack on his trading post at Sun River Crossing and his close relationship with the Kainai or Blood Blackfoot from British America:

The Death of Many Braids

On the 5th of February 1869, there were camped at Sun River Crossing three lodges of Blood Indians, the family of a Chief called "Many Braids." They were peaceably disposed, and had come from the North to trade what robes they had and to make their Spring hunt along the valley, small game being abundant. The valley had but few settlers at this time....A Diamond R train was, however, fitting up, preparatory to start for the head of navigation as soon as the freighting season opened, and the 13th Infantry, stationed at Fort Shaw, assisted to enliven the settlement at times, and the Fort was supposed to be a safe protection against all the hostile Indians in the country. The soldiers at the post had been paid off a day or two previous and a number of the men were at the [Sun River] Crossing enjoying themselves on the day of the occurrence which forms the subject of this sketch.

Many Braids and his party consisted of five men, seven women and four children and they had about forty horses among them. As war parties of Indians hostile to the Bloods were numerous in that vicinity, the Chief took the precaution to have the animals secured in the Healy Bros' corral, and on the night of the 5th they moved their camp from the point of timber below the Sun river bridge to an open space close to the buildings on the other side of the road. It happened that John J. Kennedy and John McCune were stopping with the Healys (that is myself and family) this same night, which increased the number of men in the house to eight. I visited Many Braids' lodge, accompanied by Vielle, the interpreter, and remained until nearly midnight listening to tales of heroic deeds and adventures. While in the midst of an interesting story we were startled by the sudden and vigorous howling of the dogs outside the lodges. Many Braids at once smothered the fire with ashes while Vielle and I left the lodge and went into the house, but without seeing or hearing anything to cause further alarm. It had been my custom before retiring for the night, to examine the corral and stables and see that the horses were secured, but on this occasion, I considered the Indians sufficient guard against any foes who might be lurking about in quest of plunder, and therefore neglected to make my usual rounds.

I retired soon after returning to the house, but while sitting up in bed, reading, the dogs began howling louder than ever. Several times I was on the point of turning out to investigate the cause of the unearthly noise, but for some unaccountable reason I could not make up my mind to get out of bed, and at last I turned down the light and fell asleep. I had slept perhaps half an hour, hardly more, when I was awakened by the most horrifying Indian yells mingled with the rapid discharge of firearms. Mrs. H. and the baby were the first out of bed, seeking a safe place to hide, while for the moment I was too confused to think of either flight or defense.

My first impression, after I had collected my thoughts sufficiently to think at all was that the Bloods had got whisky aboard and were having a free fight amongst themselves, and without waiting to consider further upon the subject I opened the store door. It came very near being the last act of my life. I was met by a flash of fire that blinded me and a report that for the moment left me completely senseless. An Indian lying in wait at one side of the door had discharged his pistol at my head just as I appeared at the opening. Fortunately for me, the redskin was a little too eager and a second too quick with his weapon, and although the powder burned my face, the bullet passed harmlessly by and lodged in the casing of the door.

The inmates of the house were now fully aroused, and every man had his weapon ready for attack or defense and was groping about in the dark to obtain the most serviceable position. Some person incautiously stuck a light, which immediately caused a shower of bullets to come crashing through the windows from all sides of the house, and we judged from this that the attack was made by a large party of hostile Indians intent upon finishing every one of us. As the light was extinguished, Joe Healy, who was armed with a heavy rifle and had taken up a position in one of the rear rooms of the building, saw an Indian in the act of raising the window sash. It was the last window that unhappy redskin ever meddled with, for Joe centered him neatly and the warrior dropped dead without a groan.

The attack upon the house was so sudden and unexpected that no time was allowed us to arrange any plan for defense, but fortunately the men within the building were not strangers to this kind of work, and though taken by surprise, they were not frightened nor even disposed to act merely on the defensive. Most of the men got out of the house as quickly as possible and began exchanging shots with the Indians, marking the latter by the flash of their guns.

Kennedy, McCune, Tom Healy and myself were in front of the house, loading and discharging our pieces as rapidly as we could, while the other men were stationed at different points around the building. The attacking Indians had surrounded the Bloods' camp and delivered their fire at close range, powder-burning the lodges and killing six of the inmates. Many Braids was standing close within his lodge door, and would have been rescued a moment later, but hearing our voices he thought to escape by making a dash past his enemies and reaching the house. Unfortunately for him, two of the foes were crouched on either side of the lodge door and, as the Chief came out in a stooping position, to avoid the flying bullets, one of the Indians shot him in the breast, the ball tearing its way through flesh and bone and passing out above the kidneys, taking a part of the lung with it. The Indian who fired the shot, however, made a target of himself by the flash of his pistol, and a rifle ball from one of our party fixed his flint before he had time to learn the effect of his own shot.

Meanwhile, in their eagerness to inflict all the damage possible upon the enemy, the members of our party had become so mixed up with the Indians that it was difficult to tell friend from foe. To avoid shooting each other, a few of us had withdrawn inside the house and slammed the door shut just as poor Many Braids, in his fearfully wounded condition, came running up, and finding the door closed upon him, the poor wretch began begging us to let him in, which we of course did on recognizing his voice. A ludicrous scene followed, which none of us could help laughing at in spite of our pity for the wounded Chief. As the door opened Many Braids fell into the arms of Veille, the interpreter, who happened to be in the right position to receive him. Veille was a most arrant coward and an exceedingly nervous and excitable Frenchman, and when the Chief fell upon him he probably thought his last moment had come, and began yelling murder in several languages. Many Braids clung to him with a death grip and the screaming Frenchman was unable to loosen his hold, while the rest of the party could do nothing but enjoy the circus. The struggle lasted until the Indian fell exhausted, leaving Veille covered with the blood that spurted from the wound in his breast.

We now left the house again and renewed the fight outside. The attacking party were now at work upon the corral, and were evidently having trouble with the gate, as the blows of an ax cutting away the barrier would be plainly heard. Kennedy and I secreted ourselves behind a log, within twenty feet of the corral, and could see the horses surging against the gate as the

Indians among them were throwing ropes over their necks and urging them against the enclosure to make them break through. Presently the gate came down with a crash and the animals nearly trampled upon us in their rush to get away. Two of the Indians came out mounted, and we let them have the contents of our rifles, breaking the leg of one and hitting the other in the back.

It was now our turn to make a rush in order to save at least some of the horses, and we succeeded so well that the Indians withdrew in disgust, leaving us in peace to examine at will the extent of the damage done.

Poor Many Braids was still alive when we returned to the house, and when spoken to he got up and complained of being cold. We made him as comfortable as possible, but at daylight he departed for the spirit land. His squaw was found in the lodge with a bullet in her heart, and a small infant in her arms which had been shot through the brain. His boy, about seven years old, was found wounded in the thigh, and a little girl about four years old had her eye pierced by an arrow, the weapon having passed through the eye and temple, leaving the brain protruding from the wound. The child's shoulder was also partly shot away, and altogether she was the most horrible sight I ever witnessed. When found, she was sitting in the lodge, screaming with agony, while her sister, a little blind child, was endeavoring to comfort her with kind words. One old squaw was shot while going into the house, and fell dead without shedding a drop of blood. Another squaw was wounded in the leg, and two bucks were found in the rear of the building, one was quite dead and the other lived only until morning.

Jim Matkin, who was in charge of the Diamond R train, on the other side of the river, had started an express to Fort Shaw for assistance when the fight commenced, but it was four hours after that the gallant 13th [Infantry] arrived at the scene of the fight. Dr. Hitz, the post surgeon, condescended to examine the wounded, but said there was nothing he could do for them. The child with the arrow in her head he pronounced beyond all hope of recovery, and refused to assist her in any way. That child is alive today, nature having proved a better physician than Dr. [Rudolph B.] Hitz.

The attacking party of Indians were Flatheads and Spokane, as we afterward learned.[19]

2

A VENGEFUL INVASION

FORT WHOOP-UP
AND THE WHOOP-UP TRAIL

Johnny Healy was on a mission of revenge as he crossed the Medicine Line in early January 1870. He was the first Fort Benton free trader to lead an expedition into the North West Territory of the new Dominion of Canada. This bold undertaking broke the fur/robe trading monopoly of the mighty Hudson Bay Company, which for two centuries was dominant from great Slave Lake to the present Montana northern boundary line. Thus began the Whoop-Up era, a new period in the transnational history of northern Montana and the prairie provinces of Canada, an era that would last for more than a decade, open up new settlements and end with the arrival of the Canadian Pacific Railway in 1883.

Adventurer John J. Healy, his partner Alfred B. Hamilton and eleven wagon trains departed Healy's Sun River Trading Post on the north bank of the Sun in secrecy and mild weather from Chinook winds just after Christmas on December 28, 1869, on their epic northward journey. The Healy-Hamilton expedition included John J. Healy and his brother Joseph Healy; partner Alfred B. Hamilton; George Hammond; Patrick Heaney; George Houk; John Largent; Joseph Wei; Joseph Spearson; Martin Donovan; Black teamster Bob Mills; Mexican Jose "Castilian or Spanish Joe" Aranna; and two métis, Jerry Potts and George Star, as hunters. Along with them were Big Plume and members of his band of Kainai Blood Blackfoot, adding not only protection but also confirmation that Healy's trading expedition enjoyed approval of the Bloods, whose historic territory was their destination.[20]

Left: Adventurer John J. Healy, soldier, miner and trader, in his prime. *Overholser Historical Research Center*.

Right: Healy's partner and namesake for Fort Hamilton, the new trading post, A.B. Hamilton. *Overholser Historical Research Center*.

Following the Riplinger Trail, the party moved slowly, trading along the way, traveling 160 miles over a three-week period before arriving by January 17, 1870, at the mouth of the confluence of the St. Mary's River where it joined the Belly River (south of today's Lethbridge, Alberta). The men immediately began to cut down trees to begin constructing a trading post. The design was a square structure fort containing six rooms, with three each on the east and west walls. This crude fort provided both trading and living quarters for the men. It was christened Fort Hamilton, and winter trade began very quickly with the Blood Blackfoot residents in the area.[21]

While most of the men were engaged in building the trading post, Healy and Hamilton with some Bloods searched for the highly influential Blood chief Many Spotted Horses at his winter camp near the Belly River. After giving gifts to the chief, Healy received a "winter wife," thought to be a daughter of the chief. Critically, Healy received permission to build their trading post among the Bloods.[22]

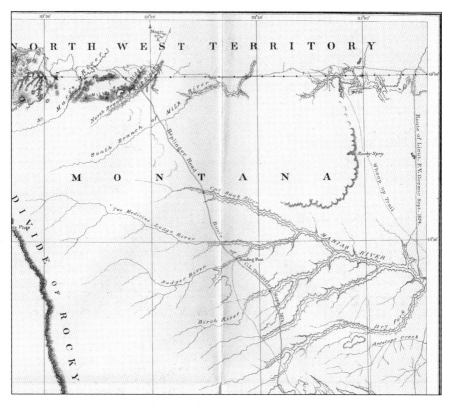

U.S. Northern Boundary Commission Survey Map No. 1 showing Whoop-Up Country and the Riplinger Trail and the western portion of the Whoop-Up Trail. *Author's collection.*

Fort Hamilton, crude and just a beginning, was underway. Through the bold actions of Healy and Hamilton, Fort Benton free traders had pried open the door to the former Rupert's Land.

HOW HAD THIS HAPPENED?

The path forward had not been easy, with many obstacles in the way throughout the fall of 1869 as Healy and Hamilton moved their plans forward. With trading, and perhaps prospecting, on their minds, the partners formed the Saskatchewan Mining, Prospecting and Trading Outfit. Healy arranged financial backing by Tom C. Power, a newly arrived Fort Benton merchant with big plans, while Hamilton may have secured some support

Above: A rare photo of the North West Fur Company Trading Post at Fort Benton taken in 1868 by Scout Charles K. Bucknum. *Overholser Historical Research Center.*

Right: T.C. Power, merchant prince who served as a U.S. senator for Montana. *Overholser Historical Research Center.*

from his uncle Isaac G. Baker, whose trading company was well on its way to becoming the leading merchant at Fort Benton.

During the fall of 1869, trader John Riplinger had warned Francis H. Eastman, head of the weakening North West Fur Company and successor to the American Fur Company on the Upper Missouri, that "a party [was] going to leave Benton to go to the [British] Territory mines to prospect for Gold." Eastman, in turn, raised red flags, advising U.S. marshal William F. Wheeler of Healy and Hamilton's trading of liquor to the Indians at their Sun River Crossing trading post and their planned activities to lead "all the old Indian Whiskey traders…on a regular whiskey trade this winter" in the British possessions.[23]

When Healy and Hamilton departed Sun River on December 28, their announced intention was to prospect for gold and silver across the Medicine Line, yet just as Eastman had warned, their real intention was to establish a trading post with the Canadian Blackfoot tribes in the Belly River country. Another critical step was to gain permission to pass through the Blackfeet reservation in Montana. Irish John Healy, active in the Choteau County Democratic Party, apparently called on his political ally, Montana territorial delegate James Cavanaugh, in Washington to use his clout to direct Montana superintendent of Indian affairs General Alfred Sully to provide the permit. General Sully complied by issuing this handwritten permit:

PERMIT TO MESSRS. HAMILTON HEALY TO TRAVEL THROUGH THE BLACKFOOT COUNTRY

Messrs. A.B. Hamilton and J.J. Healy of Montana Territory having placed in my honor bonds and security to the amount of $10,000 that they will not trade with any person neither white men, negroes or Indians in this Territory after they leave Sun River Settlement—and being satisfied that said persons have no intentions to infringe the laws regulating trade and intercourse with the Indians and by direction of the Commissioner of Indian Affairs at Washington permitted to pass through the Blackfoot Country and cross the northern boundary line of the United States of America at a point within about 30 miles of St. Mary's Lake. They are also privileged to take with them a party of 20 to 30 men and six wagons loaded with supplies provided there is no spiritous liquors in the Wagons except a small quantity which may be taken safely for medicinal purposes. Not to exceed [quantity vacant].

Alf Sully

U.S.A.

Supt Inds.[24]

The Healy and Hamilton trading operation was underway, under the guise of a mining expedition. In his *Frontier Sketches #34*, Johnny Healy wrote his impression of "The Indian Traders":

Among certain classes of people, the name of Indian trader is synonymous with everything disreputable. The villainous traders are the cause of our Indian wars. They excite the Indians with whiskey and then furnish them with ammunition to defy the efforts of the Government to keep them in subjugation. These kindred expressions are frequently found in Eastern journals, and they have led the uninitiated to believe that any man, who can have commercial transactions with the untutored red, must be a monster of hideous form and most revolting aspect.

The truth is, however, that the traders have done more towards subduing the evil propensities of the Indians than all the soldiers

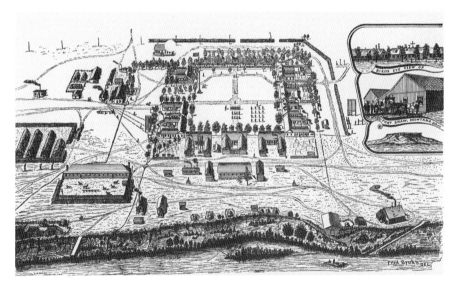

Bird's-eye view of Fort Shaw, built in 1867, about six miles upriver from Sun River Crossing. *Author's collection.*

Marias River site of the massacre of Heavy Runner's Camp of Blackfeet in January 1870. Photo taken about 1882 by A.B. Coe. *Overholser Historical Research Center.*

and agents of the government have yet accomplished, and if the sale of whiskey and ammunition has excited the Indian to deeds or bloodshed and enabled him to gratify his desire for plunder and butchery, the traders themselves have usually been the only victims of his fiendish inclinations.

The traders are, or at least were before the settlement of the Territories, considered the friends and allies of the tribes with which they dealt and were regarded as enemies by the tribes with which they did not deal. A trader, for example, who dealt with the Gros Ventres, was protected by that tribe, but was treated as an enemy by any tribe with which the Gros Ventres were at war, and as it was frequently necessary for the trader to pass through the country of his enemies in order to procure his goods and return to his customers, the dangers which he was often obliged to encounter making his calling extremely dangerous and frequently unprofitable.

It is therefore evident, that the traders themselves were more likely to become victims of Indian hostility than were any other of the white inhabitants of the frontier, and…so far from being the causes of Indian wars they were the…most efficient protectors of the settlements.[25]

THE MARIAS TRAGEDY

Just weeks after the Healy-Hamilton expedition crossed the Marias River on its way north, U.S. Army cavalry and infantry departed Fort Shaw, just seven miles from Sun River Crossing, on an expedition that would rock the Upper Missouri region and have a profound and lasting effect on the Blackfoot Nation. On the morning of January 19, a punitive army force of 380 men departed Fort Shaw, including Troops F, G, H and I of the U.S. Second Cavalry from Fort Ellis with 55 mounted infantry and Companies A and L from the Thirteenth Infantry from Fort Shaw. With Major Eugene Baker, Second Cavalry, in command, their mission was to "strike hard" the village of Piegan Blackfeet Mountain Chief in retaliation for multiple incidents along the Benton to Helena Road, culminating in the stunning murder of trader/rancher Malcolm Clarke in August 1869.

The Baker command, guided by scouts Joe Kipp, Joseph Cobell and Horace Clarke, son of the murdered Malcolm, and recovering from his own near fatal wound, moved northward toward the Blackfeet winter camps on the Marias River in sub-zero temperatures through one to two feet of snow, and by the night of January 22, they were in position for an early morning strike. Meanwhile, Kipp, Cobell and Clarke scouted ahead to find the location of Mountain Chief's band, only to learn that Mountain Chief had moved his camp nine miles downriver after receiving a warning of impending army action.

Despite urgent pleading by Kipp and the other scouts, Major Baker proceeded directly to attack the closest camp, the wrong camp, that of the smallpox-stricken band of Chief Heavy Runner. In the brutal slaughter that followed, some 217 Piegans, including Heavy Runner and many women and children, were slain.[26]

This tragedy, the Marias Massacre, happened just weeks after the Healy-Hamilton expedition had passed through the area. Later, on February 6, John Healy returned to Sun River Crossing and learned for the first time about the "late expedition." The *Helena Herald* reported on his arrival:

> John Healy arrived at Sun River Crossing today from the new trading store that he and Al Hamilton started a short time since on the Belly River, in the British Possessions. He says that they are doing very well out there, reports all things quiet, did not see any Indians, nor even hear of the late expedition until he arrived here, and does not believe that there is one word of truth in the

reports that are going the rounds about the Indians having taken their squaws and papooses over to the other side of the line, but is of the opinion that the fate of Bear Chief's band will have a very salutary effect upon our red-skinned brethren and cause them to keep shady for a time at least.[27]

A Clash of Cultures

In early March 1870, a mass meeting assembled in Helena to support the strong military action by Major Baker. A local committee reported that during the past five years some two hundred White men had been massacred and two thousand horses stolen by Indians in northern Montana Territory. The *Helena Herald* reported on the meeting:

Public Meeting at the Court House

The citizens' meeting at the Court House Saturday night was largely attended and harmonious. Col. W.F. Sanders presided. The committee appointed at a previous meeting to gather facts and data relating to Indian depredations, reported that during the past five years about two hundred white men had been massacred and upwards of two thousand horses stolen by the different tribes within this Territory. Judge [Cornelius] Hedges reported the following preamble and resolutions, which were unanimously adopted:

WHEREAS, Much severe and unjust censure is indulged in and circulated in the East against Col. Baker and the troops under his command engaged in the recent chastisement of the Peigan Indians on the Marias in this Territory, and

WHEREAS, We are convinced that those censures are based upon a misrepresentation of facts, and still more upon a misunderstanding of the true Indian character, therefore be it

Resolved. By the citizens of Montana in mass meeting assembled, and after diligently seeking all the information concerning the so-called massacre attainable, and carefully comparing and reviewing the same.

That in our judgement the long continued, oft-repeated acts of murder and pillage committed by the tribe of Indians,

Colonel Wilbur Fisk
Sanders, vigilante
prosecutor, later
U.S. senator from
Montana.
Author's collection.

culminating in the murder of one of our oldest and most respected citizens, the late Malcolm Clarke, under circumstances of peculiar atrocity and treachery, demanded signal and exemplary punishment.

That the cowardly nature of the Indian renders it necessary to seek him in his camp among his squaws and children, when confined by the rigors of the season, and fight him in the style that he alone recognizes and practices.

That in our opinion it is the first duty of the Government to protect its own citizens at any cost; to encourage the hardy adventurer who seeks to develop the resources of the country and assure to him safety in person, property, and family; that whatever severity of retaliation is necessary to this end should not be accounted barbarity but is in reality kindness to those who deserve it.

That in our opinion Col. Baker and his command discharged a disagreeable duty faithfully and deserve the gratitude of the whole country, as they receive that of every good citizen of Montana, who can now breathe, sleep and travel with a full sense of security than ever before since he entered the Territory.

That the only class of our citizens who complain of cruelty are those who cluster around the agencies and whose gains arise

Top: Golden Jubilee edition of the *Lethbridge Herald* featuring "Fort Whoop-Up, Cradle of White Man's Civilization in Southern Alberta Territory." *From the* Lethbridge Herald, *July 11, 1935.*

Bottom: Blackfeet warriors on parade. *Author's collection.*

from the sale of whisky and ammunition to the Indians, and who are equally guilty of the crimes they commit.

That it is the duty of our Government to interpose to prevent the so-called trading posts in British America from encouraging and supplying the Indians to their thieving and murdering expeditions upon our citizens, and for this purpose we ask the cooperation of our Delegate in Congress.

That we disclaim all cruel and vindictive feeling against the Indians, but as all the past history of our country has shown him to be a horse thief and a murderer by inclination and education, we believe our Government should rigidly confine him to reservations and compel him to cultivate the soil and earn his bread as the Lord has commanded by the sweat of his brow.[28]

BUILDING FORT HAMILTON

In later years, one of John Healy's men, Patrick Heaney, reminisced about the early days at Fort Hamilton and the tension in the aftermath of the Marias Massacre. Heaney's story, told to Mrs. J.C. Taylor of Bynum, appeared in the *Dillon Examiner* under the dramatic headline "Healy and Hamilton Faced Death When 500 Blood Braves Stood between Few White Traders and Vengeful Piegans."

The last twenty years has seen the departure from our midst of most of the real, old-time frontiersmen who were still to be found in Montana, holdovers of a bygone day, when I came to the state a score of years ago. Among the few that I knew there were some interesting men who could tell thrilling tales if they were disposed to loosen their tongues. Occasionally two or three of these grizzled veterans of the wilderness, who had seen more real action in a month than the average man of today sees in a lifetime, would get together before a fire. Then, one incident recalling another, they would forget the present and once more travel the trails of the past. It was on such an occasion that an old Irishman, Pat Heaney, told a true yarn of an adventure at a trading post in Canada, across from the Montana line, that I can tell again now, because I made notes of names and dates and the principal incidents related. All of the men involved are long since dead.

Heaney, so his story went, was a young man when he was mustered out of the army in 1865 at the Crocondelet barracks in St. Louis and joined a company of 47 men bound for the gold diggings in Idaho. Traveling to Fort Leavenworth, the outfit bought necessary provisions, mules, and wagons at the army depot, and headed across the plains. Increasing the size of their party to make the expedition safe, they finally reached Fort Laramie, where they heard of the latest big strike in Montana—at Last Chance Gulch, where Helena was built. They decided to go there, and traveling to Gallatin City, they crossed the Missouri near Three Forks.

They got to Last Chance on July 4, 1866, and found a noisy miners' celebration going on.

Heaney tried prospecting on Silver creek, and shortly drifted on down to Sun River Crossing, where he met two famous Indian traders who were well known in early-day Montana history. These were Al. Hamilton and Captain John J. Healy, both sheriffs of Chouteau county later. The three became close friends and decided to organize an expedition to travel north to trade with the Indians in Canada, in what was known as Rupert's Land—now the Northwest Territories of Canada. They left Sun River during the week after Christmas, 1869, locating three weeks later at the forks of Belly river and St. Mary's river. The trading post they built there they called Fort Whoop-Up....

It happened that as they were crossing the Marias river on their way north, they ran into a party of 20 Blood Indians, who were hungry because they had run out of a game country. The three men took these Bloods along with them, feeding them until they struck into a band of buffalo again. [According to George Houk, the leader of this band of Bloods was Buffalo Bull's Back Fat, a hereditary chief with powerful standing.[29]]

The Bloods appreciated what had been done for them and urged the trio to build a post for trading....

Before the stockade was finished, however, along came a great band of Piegans under the leadership of Cut Hand. When the advance of this party rode up, Heaney, Healy and Hamilton were cooking in an Indian lodge. Into this ran an old Blood squaw, her tongue rattling in terror like a fire bell, for she feared the Piegans would kill the whitemen at once. She knew that some of the Blackfeet bands, including these Piegans, were very bitter over the massacre of Heavy Runner's smallpox camp on the Marias river shortly before, when Major Eugene M. Baker and his cavalry butchered in cold blood hundreds of helpless women, children and old people who had done no wrong.

"Cut Hand is here," she shouted. "He will trade only for powder and ball. When he gets enough he will kill you three white men, as well as the other five at the stockade."

Healey, Heaney and Hamilton were nervous over the prospect, but they did not become "stampeded." While they were discussing the situation, Mart Dunraven, a wagon boss for

Hugh Kirkendall, wandered over to the lodge and suggested that he would like something to eat. "If I'm going to cash in," he said, "I want a full stomach to die on."

"You can do as you please," remarked Healy, "but I'm going to get behind those logs," and he started for the stockade, which stood partly finished fifty yards away. The walls were up, but the buildings within were not completed. The rest of the party followed Healy inside the fort, where there were plenty of needle guns and "fixed" ammunition. Their axes soon had the ammunition boxes open, and each man stationed himself where he could do the most execution in the event of an attack, which they looked for every minute.

Healy, Hamilton and a man known as Jose remained in the partly-finished trading room, determined to sell their lives at as much cost to the Piegans as possible. There they halted for perhaps 15 minutes before a sudden knock came at the door. After some hesitation they decided to open up, and when they did there stood the war chief of their friends, the Bloods, stripped for battle. His name was [Buffalo] Bull's Back Fat, and he was a fine specimen of an Indian warrior. He entered, signed to close the door and then sat down on a powder box for fully five minutes before uttering a word.

At last he said: "Friends, you know the white soldiers a short time ago cleaned out the Piegan camp over on the Marias. There were no warriors in that camp, for it was a 'sick camp,' and the able-bodied men were out hunting for meat for their wives, babies and old people. The white soldiers came in the night and slaughtered the sick old men and women, the mothers and the babies as they slept or hunted them down in the snow and killed them. The hearts of all the Blackfeet, the Piegans and Bloods are filled with bitterness against the whites for this. Cut Hand and his Piegans have come here to kill you.

"But you men have been kind to us and you are our traders. We Bloods were hungry when you met us and fed us. We are grateful. Now five hundred of my warriors have joined our party. The Piegans will have to kill us before they kill you. They outnumber us greatly, but they are our cousins, and I do not believe they will force us to fight. If they do, we will die fighting for you white men. Open the door and look out."

Hamilton opened the door of the trading room and saw the fort completely surrounded by Blood warriors, stripped for fighting. Some had guns; others were armed with bows and arrows, stone war clubs, spears and hatchets. Beyond, standing excitedly talking in groups, were hundreds of Piegan warriors, evidently angry and vengeful. The eight white men felt the tenseness of the moment. They expected hell to break loose, as Heaney expressed it.

The Blood chief, Bull's Back Fat, stepped out and addressed the Piegans, signing for them to start the trade. They lined up, every man carrying weapons of some sort, and each one accompanied by a squaw or two laden with furs and buffalo robes. The Blood chief admitted only two at a time to the fort to trade, but little time was lost. Instead of the usual barter, of the furs and robes for cloth blankets, tobacco, beads, calico and other trade articles used by the reds, the Piegans all threw down their robes and demanded powder and lead. The white men gave them at first forty rounds of powder and ball for one robe, but as the supply of ammunition dwindled, they cut down to twenty rounds and finally to ten rounds. They expected a protest but none was made.

The last to trade was Cut Hand, the Piegan chief, and as he finished, the white men saw that the crisis was at hand. It was, for as the Piegan chief started out of the door, Bull's Back Fat stopped him. "You have finished trading with these white men," he said. "Now go and go peacefully. You have come to kill these white men. You will have to kill me and my men first. If I find that later you molest these friends of mine, I will attack your camp. You will be the first I will kill."

Cut Hand stalked out of the fort and briefly ordered his band to break camp and start north. It took two and a half hours for them to pass a given point, Heaney told me.

After they had gone the white traders started cooking a feast for the Bloods, and they made merry till Heaney said they took 1,600 buffalo robes and many furs and elk hides in this trade.[30]

END OF TRADING SEASON

Winter trading proved beyond Healy's hopes, as Blood and Peigan arrived at Fort Hamilton to exchange their robes, hides and furs for tobacco, salt, sugar, flour, tea, axes, knives, blankets, calico, wire, beads and silver trinkets—in addition to repeating rifles, ammunition and whisky. Smallpox, brought from the southern Piegan tribes to the northern Blood and Peigan during that winter of 1869–70, raged and then peaked by the end of the winter, causing the death of about six hundred in each tribe, with similar losses among the Cree, Assiniboine and Gros Ventres. In the words of historian Rodger D. Touchie, "What the White man's guns and whiskey had failed to complete in seven years, disease had done in seven months."[31]

As the winter trading season ended, Healy and Hamilton prepared to depart with some fifteen thousand bison robes and other hides and furs to market at Fort Benton in time for the spring steamboat arrivals. As they departed Fort Hamilton, a fire destroyed part of the trading post. Accounts of the fire vary, yet most likely the Blackfoot burned the post after the traders departed.

Howell Harris was one of the bullwhackers in the Healy-Hamilton train that hauled the rich winter trade to Fort Benton. Born in 1845 in St. Louis, Harris moved west with his parents into the Idaho country; in 1863, at age seventeen, he stampeded into the placer mines of Montana. Harris moved on to Fort Benton and became one of the many larger-than-life Whoop-Up characters, working for William G. and Charles E. Conrad trading and ranching before returning to Montana. Howell Harris shared his memories of Whoop-Up Country:

Howell Harris—First Trip to Canada

My first trip into Canada was in the fall of 1869....A band of Blackfeet Indians had stolen some stock belonging to James Coburn so I and two bullwhackers followed them as far as Milk River, just north of the Sweet Grass Hills. During our trip, we came across countless herds of buffalo. We did not recover the horses, cattle or work oxen, however, as the Indians were too numerous and warlike, so we returned to Fort Benton.

My next trip was in the spring of [1870] from Fort Benton to Fort Whoop-Up, at the forks of St. Mary's and Belly rivers. This was the first fort built in Alberta south of Edmonton. I was sent

Charles E. Conrad, partner in I.G. Baker & Co., managed most of the firm's operations in Canada over the years. *Overholser Historical Research Center.*

with a bull train to collect furs traded for during the previous winter by Healy and Hamilton, who built the fort. During this trip the Blood Indians shot a Frenchman belonging to our train, this occurring near the fort.

Just after we started on our return trip, nobody being left in the fort except a sick squaw, the Indians set fire to the fort. We forded the St. Mary's and camped where the station of St. Mary's is at present. Mr. Hamilton and I returned to try and save the squaw but we found the Indians shot her before setting fire to the fort. Our return trip was without further incident, although we had to be on guard constantly. Hamilton and Healy rebuilt the fort the same summer.[32]

Healy, Hamilton and Howell Harris's bull train arrived at Fort Benton in late spring with their winter's trade. Their triumphant return was announced in the *Helena Herald* of June 15:

Successful Venture

It will be remembered last winter, Messrs. Al. Hamilton and John Healy, two of Sun River's enterprising citizens, having

Bull train loaded at Fort Benton, heading out for Whoop-Up Country. Photo by W.E. Hook. *Overholser Historical Research Center.*

Overview of Fort Whoop-Up on the Belly River, likely taken by traveling photographer W.E. Hook in 1878. *Overholser Historical Research Center.*

Second Fort Whoop-Up, built by William Gladstone and Metís carpenters during the fall of 1870. *Overholser Historical Research Center.*

received authorization to go beyond the border to trade for robes, departed with their outfit of Indian goods into the British Possessions. These gentlemen recently returned from their expedition, bringing with them a large number of robes and peltries of various kinds. Mr. Largent, whom we had the pleasure of meeting at Sun River, on Saturday, informs us that his trip had not been altogether unpleasant or entirely unsatisfactory in its pecuniary benefits. We judge, from all we could learn, that this venture will net Messrs. Hamilton and Healy upwards of $50,000—not so very bad for a six months' cruise…across the border.[33]

A New Fort Hamilton

With their financial success, Healy and Hamilton were able to make T.C. Power's investment profitable for him. A priority for Healy and Hamilton on their arrival at Fort Benton was to hire William Gladstone, a carpenter formerly with the Hudson Bay Company, to build a new Fort Hamilton large enough to withstand any sort of assault that could be made on it. Gladstone left in June with his construction crew of forty men, primarily Canadian Métis. While the fort would take two years to complete, Gladstone's men partially completed the elaborate new outpost by the time Healy and Hamilton returned in the fall to allow trading and living through the winter.[34]

Building the new Fort Hamilton, soon known to all as Fort Whoop-Up, was a major project. Located southwest and nearby the original fort, the new trading fort took six thousand hewn and squared cottonwood logs. Two bastions on the northeast and southwest corners, designed to cover all four walls, bore a mounted two-inch muzzle-loading bronze cannon on a gun carriage and a six-pounder mountain howitzer, brought from Fort Benton. Both bastions were supplied with plenty of grape and canister shot in the shape of twenty-five-pound sacks of trade balls.

The upright timber walls of the palisade were chinked with mud with loopholes for muskets, ramparts, heavy gates and a smaller gate to allow entry for a horse and rider. Buildings were positioned along the entire length of the north and west walls and a portion of the south wall. Building sections housed dwellings, a blacksmith shop, storerooms, a stable, the kitchen, robe storage and a long trade room with a high, solid counter.[35]

A saloon in the fort was manned by Sol Abbott, and this was the scene, on occasion, of some rough incidents, as described in the *Helena Herald* of April 1873. This account brings the first news that the British were preparing to send troops to "the Whoop-Up country":

> Some ten days since [in February] there occurred a fight at this point which resulted in seriously wounding three white men and the killing of three Indians. The provocation to the fight we are not informed of, and we therefore simply give a report of the struggle as related to us by gentlemen just up from the lower country.
>
> At the time mentioned, three white men named Kanouse, Lafleur and Horness were in the saloon of a Mr. Abbott, when a band of Blackfeet Indians walked into the room and shot them down and then proceeded to help themselves to liquor. The proprietor, who happened at the time to be in the back room, at this juncture opened the door and proceeded with his navy [revolver] to lay out the Indians in lively style. With the first three shots he killed as many foes, and the balance fled precipitately. Examination showed that Kanouse had his shoulder blown away, the muzzle of the gun having been placed against it when fired, leaving a most shocking and fatal wound. Lafleur was shot through the thigh, and Horness through the hand and side; both will probably recover. An ambulance was sent up from Benton

after the wounded men, which has doubtless arrived back with them before this.

There is a report current at Benton, and we trust it may be verified, that the British government are going to send a company of troops to this Whoop-Up country this spring. Nothing short of this will ever stop the illegal traffic there going on, or bring safety to the lives or property of the residents.[36]

Life at Fort Whoop-Up from 1870 to 1874 followed the seasonal trading cycle: winter and early spring trading, movement of robes and furs to Fort Benton in the late spring, with traders returning with their trade goods in the fall to begin the new winter trading cycle. In 1935, the *Lethbridge Herald* critically described the Fort Whoop-Up era:

Fort Whoop-Up, Cradle of White Man's Civilization in Southern Alberta Territory

Fort Benton, about eight days away by bull team, some 200 miles, was the birthplace of Fort Whoop-Up in South Alberta. In those last days of the buffalo, we are told, large numbers of reckless traders entered South Alberta, did as they pleased, ruined the Indians with whiskey, built strong forts and established a reign of brigandage and murder. Whiskey was traded, to the great advantage of the trader, for buffalo, wolf, and other skins. Goods to be exchanged for the fur were brought in without duty, and the whole trade was carried on in defiance of the laws of Canada and the United States.

Healy and Hamilton

It is such an era of our history that two notorious characters, Healy and Hamilton, decided to establish a fort in South Alberta territory, drawing their supplies from Fort Benton, and clearing their skins and furs south through Fort Benton. It is stated there were two Healys, John and Joe....However, the name of the fort was Fort Hamilton, after one of the partners. It was built in [1870].

At first the fort was not strongly built, and so wild became the orgies staged by the Indians about its walls that, in 1871, according to Howell Harris, famous frontiersman, Indian trader and cattleman of Fort Benton and Lethbridge, the Indians burned Fort Hamilton to the ground after killing a squaw who had been inside with the traders before they escaped to safety. Mr. Harris tells us the fort was rebuilt by Healy and Hamilton the same summer, 1871.

John D. Higginbotham in his book, "When the West was Young," throws some light on how Fort Hamilton became Fort Whoop-Up. He tells how, on one occasion, a trader returned to Fort Benton from Fort Hamilton and, when asked how things were when he left he said; "O, they're still a-whoopin' of 'er up." And so, Fort Hamilton came to be known as Fort Whoop-Up, and the colorful name stuck, so that when the Mounted Police "Originals" reached the confluence of the Belly and the St. Mary Rivers in 1874 on their trek across the southern prairies to establish law and order, it was Fort Whoop-Up they saw nestled under the bank.

Life at Whoop-Up

Describing life there in the early days, Chief "Joe" Healy, [son of Many Braids,] step-son of [John] Healy who with Hamilton established Fort Whoop-Up, recently told a *Herald* correspondent who visited him on the Blood Reserve.

"The Fort Whoop-Up days were dangerous and uncertain. Every vice and crime was practiced there. The Indian camps were alight with dance and all forms of savage practice and crime. The white traders in those days were mere gamblers.... But when the Mounted Police appeared in the territory in 1874 the great leaders and the dangerous conditions subdued.

The trader stood at a wicket, a tub full of whiskey beside him, and when an Indian pushed a buffalo robe to him through the hole, he handed out a tin cup full of the poisonous decoction. A quart of the stuff bought a fine pony. When the spring came, wagon loads of the traffic were escorted to Fort Benton in Montana, 200 miles away."[37]

Above: A Metís
family resting in
the shade of a
Red River cart.
Author's collection.

Right: Old North
Trail along the
Rocky Mountain
Front. *Photo by author.*

WHOOP-UP TRAIL

The Old North Trail had worn its way into history along the eastern Rocky Mountain Front by indigenous peoples for centuries. As the fur/robe trading posts began operations on the Upper Missouri from 1831 and later Euro-American settlements opened in the Sun River Valley, other trails began to form, including the Riplinger from the north to Sun River and the Fort Benton trail to the trading post on the Missouri River. All trails, north and south, passed through Blackfoot country. With the opening of Fort Whoop-Up, the Fort Benton trail became known as the Whoop-Up Trail extending some two hundred miles from Fort Benton to the prairie provinces of Canada; this trail played a profound role in the settlement history of the Montana and Canadian frontiers. From Fort Benton, massive freight from the States flowed into the river port. With the success of Healy and Hamilton, free traders by the score moved north along the trail and over the border into the newly formed North West Territory. Fort Hamilton became Fort Whoop-Up, and the trail that led there became the Whoop-Up Trail. *Great Falls Tribune* feature writer Marguerite Marmont presented the best description of the famed Whoop-Up Trail.

Old Fort Whoop-Up Trail Described by Harry Stanford

Whiskey Running Was Profitable in Days When Freighters Drove Over 230-Mile Route; Many Landmarks Remembered.

Many freight trains pulled over the Whoop-Up trail in its day. Trains drawn by oxen and mules, with crews of bullwhackers and mule skinners. Today, only those who know where to look can trace its route in faint broken scars on stretches of virgin prairie between Fort Benton and Macleod, Alta. It is clearer only in the memories of those who traveled over it until they learned every rock and rut along its 230 miles.

Harry P. Stanford of Kalispell has sketched a map showing the trail and interesting points in the surrounding country as he remembers them. He says:

"I never freighted, but I made four through trips over the Whoop-Up trail in 1884, two more in January and February, 1885, and another in October, 1886. Surely got to know every

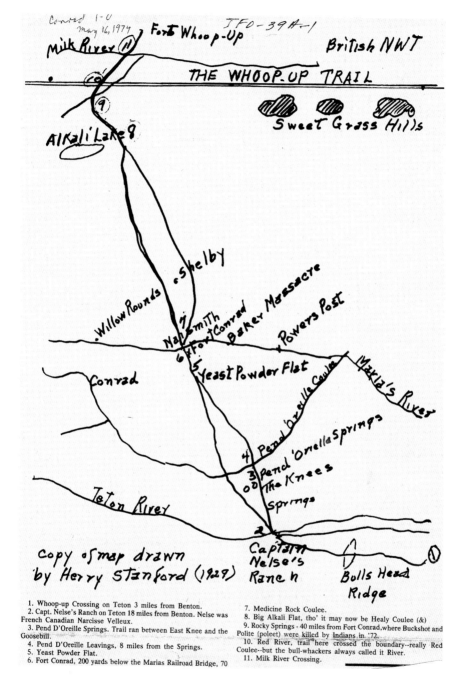

1. Whoop-up Crossing on Teton 3 miles from Benton.
2. Capt. Nelse's Ranch on Teton 18 miles from Benton. Nelse was French Canadian Narcisse Velleux.
3. Pend D'Oreille Springs. Trail ran between East Knee and the Goosebill.
4. Pend D'Oreille Leavings, 8 miles from the Springs.
5. Yeast Powder Flat.
6. Fort Conrad, 200 yards below the Marias Railroad Bridge, 70
7. Medicine Rock Coulee.
8. Big Alkali Flat, tho' it may now be Healy Coulee (&)
9. Rocky Springs - 40 miles from Fort Conrad,where Buckshot and Polite (poleet) were killed by Indians in .'72.
10. Red River, trail here crossed the boundary--really Red Coulee--but the bull-whackers always called it River.
11. Milk River Crossing.

Map drawn by Harry Stanford of the Whoop-Up Trail, from Captain Nelse to Fort Whoop-Up. *Overholser Historical Research Center.*

chuck hole on it, as one does who travels by wagon and saddle and has time to. I rode with bull, mule, even whiskey outfits, though I disclaim any role with the latter other than that of disinterested observer. Whiskey flowed north then, Alberta being dry."

Mr. Stanford came to Fort Benton in 1879 with his mother and sister, the late Mrs. Charles Conrad of Kalispell. They traveled on the steamboat "Montana," the biggest and finest boat to ascend the river that far. It was a three months' trip from Pittsburgh to Fort Benton. There they joined the late James T. Stanford, who had served with the original North West Mounted Police at Fort Macleod. In 1890 Mr. Stanford moved to the Flathead valley; in 1891, to Kalispell. He is a taxidermist.

First Prohibition Law. The Whoop-Up Trail was first used to any extent in 1870, the date of Montana's first serious attempt at prohibition enforcement. Selling whiskey to Indians had been forbidden and United States marshals and their deputies set out to see that the law was respected. Fur traders regarded whisky as the chief requisite of their business. Where whiskey was, there the trade was, they believed. So, they built posts in less restricted territory across the Canadian border.

One of the first of these trading posts was built by Capt. John J. Healy and A.B. Hamilton at the confluence of the St. Mary's and Belly rivers, eight miles from where Lethbridge now stands. It was named Fort Hamilton but flourishing business led to its rechristening.

When Johnny LaMott, one of the traders, returned from the Canadian territory, he was asked by John Power of Fort Benton: "How's business?"

"Oh, they're just whoopin' 'er up," LaMotte replied....

Trade goods had to come by boat up the Missouri and thence over the Whoop-Up trail to Canadian posts.

The trade continued in "whoop it up" until 1874. Then Fort Macleod was built by the Royal Mounted Police under Col. James T. Macleod on Old Man's river, 28 miles from Fort Whoop-Up. They were sent by the Canadian government to stop the whisky business and regulate Indian trade. Owners of older posts transferred operations once more to the United States.

Freight for the Mounted Police was shipped up the Missouri river in bond to a Canadian customs officer at Fort Benton. He

John W. Power, the "brother" in the commercial giant T.C. Power & Bro., remained in Fort Benton managing company operations after Tom Power moved to Helena. *Overholser Historical Research Center.*

let the contract for hauling it to I.G. Baker & Co., who built a trading store at Fort Macleod. Many freight trains were used for this transportation.

On the route from Fort Benton, the first camp was at Eight-Mile Springs. Then the freighters passed "Bull's Head" bridge and crossed the Teton river 18 miles from Benton at what became known as Captain Nelse's place....

Capt. Narcisse Vielleaux was a well-known character on both sides of the international line. Born near Montreal about 1830, he had come up the Missouri on the cordelle, had struck gold on Stinking Water (Ruby) creek and then settled near Fort Benton. He often went to Fort Macleod to trap and hunt in the winter and returned in the spring with wagons loaded with furs. He was popular as a scout and guide.

From the Teton, the road led past the Goosebill (Baque d'Otard) and the Knees (Genou). Farther on was Pile of Rocks, an old Indian lookout on the side of a coulee north of the road. Its elevation gave a commanding view of the surrounding country.

There was another good camping place at Pend d'Oreille Springs. "Froggie" had a stopping place there in later years.

Pend d'Oreille coulee runs from there northeast to the Marias river. From Pend d'Oreille leavings, the road stretched across Yeast Powder flat, so-called because the alkali looked so much like baking powder. It then crossed the Dry fork of the Marias and led to Fort Conrad, west of the mouth of the Dry Fork and about 70 miles from Fort Benton.

Fort Conrad consisted of a few log buildings, a storeroom, warehouse living quarters for the post trader and his family and barns and corrals During its early years there was a good trade with the Indians there. Freighters on the Whoop-Up Trail and soldiers on summer patrol duty were glad to patronize it. W.G. Conrad, A.B. Hamilton, Joe Kipp and James Willard Schultz lived there at different times....

The Willow Rounds

About 12 miles up the Marias was the Willow Rounds. An outpost had been built there by the American Fur Company in the fall of 1848, with a man named Hammel (aka Armell) in charge. At the same time this company had a post higher up the Marias at Flatwood in charge of Malcolm Clarke. Both posts were abandoned in 1856. I.G. Baker & Co. established a branch post at the Willow Rounds in 1868–69, when many furs were collected. It was discontinued the next year but another was built at Medicine Creek. "Sol" Abbott and Henry Powell kept a trading store at the Willow Rounds as late as 1882. It became a "stopping place" for cowboys and whisky runners. Abbott stayed there until he died in 1893. When neighbors moved in so close Powell could see their smoke, he moved out. They were too close to him.

Until 1878 there were many buffaloes and much other game along the Marias. The deep river bottoms provided protection and wood so the Piegans had large winter encampments there.

Power's post was built farther down the river to the "Big Bend' section. It was conducted by H.A. Nottingham for T.C. Power & Co., in 1876.

One place on the Marias river was considered "bad medicine" and always avoided by the Piegan Indians. "It Fell on Them" was their name for it. As the story was told to Mr. Stanford by Joe Kipp, once a number of Indian women were hunting for white clay, which they used to clean buckskin suits. They found a layer of it under a high cutbank but as they were getting it, the bank caved on them. They were all buried alive.

Another unfortunate location for the Indians was the scene of the Baker massacre on the Marias river in January, 1870.

Piegans' Sacred Stone

Leaving Fort Conrad, the Whoop-Up trail crossed the [Marias] river at Whoop-Up, or Macleod crossing, and then followed the Medicine Rock bottom to its head, where the road passed the rock that gave the bottom its name. It is rather an insignificant looking whitish stone, considered sacred by the Indians because it seemed to have power to move. Erosion of the sandy soil beneath caused it to gradually shift its position down a steep hillside. Whenever they passed on their travois trail, the Piegans said a prayer and left an offering. Most freighters did not hesitate to appropriate food, trinkets or furs they found there.

Past Medicine Rock, the road led up Medicine Rock coulee, where the Burlington railroad now runs. It crossed Antelope coulee just east of the present site of Shelby.

Then there were alternative routes. In dry weather freight trains swung up the long coulee that reaches from there to the Canadian border. In wet weather, when this coulee contained a long mushy lake, they followed a trail on the bench to the east. They crossed Black, Green and J.O. coulees before coming to the Red Wagon coulee, where the road traversed the alkali flat mouth of where Kevin now stands, and climbed up the ridge on the west side.

Freighters never overlooked Rocky Springs as a camping place. It was the highest point on the ridge, 40 miles from Fort Conrad.

At the foot of the slope and slightly to the northeast are the graves of Buckshot and Polite, wolfers killed by a band of Assiniboine in 1871. The bodies were found pierced with so many arrows that they looked like huge porcupines. The weather was so cold they found it necessary to burn their lodge poles to thaw the ground so graves could be dug.

Another incident of the extremely cold winter of 1871 is told in the biography of James W. Brown in Bowen's "Progressive

Fort Benton front street with cargo on levee in August 1868. Photo by C.R. Savage. *Author's collection.*

Men." In December, 1871, Brown left Fort Benton with a load of trade goods for a Canadian post. His party was overtaken by such a terrific snowstorm that sometimes they could advance only a mile a day. After reaching Rocky Springs, they were forced to remain there, protected from the storm by a skin lodge they bought from Indians at Medicine Rock for a gallon of whisky. "The cold was almost unendurable, whisky froze, coal oil became a thick slush, their horses chewed the wagon boxes and consumed a dozen brooms." The story goes. Many of the animals froze. It was Feb. 18 before the men could push on into Canada.

Halfway between Rocky Springs and Red River was Split Rock. According to a Piegan legend, Old Man, their rascally creator, was once chased there by a grizzly bear. In the nick of time a bull bat swooped down and split the rock so old Man could crawl inside to escape.

A favorite camping ground north of the border was John Joe's springs, named for the champion wolfer of the day. In 1884 the springs were two high piles of wolf heads, showing the great number of animals John Joe had skinned. He was a man of great strength and splendid physique and a hero to the freighters because he could lift a big whisky barrel and push it out waist high into a Murphy wagon. Later this place was called Tennant's springs.

Further north, after crossing Milk river, the road passed Indian rifle pits, then Ed Mann's Middle, and Kipp's coulees. After 1874 most of the travel went east of Fort Whoop Up past where Lethbridge now stands and then over Captain Jack's bottom, past Fort Thomas, Fort Kipp and Fort Weatherwax to Fort Macleod.

Freighting continued over the Whoop Up trail until 1885 when the Canadian pacific railway pushed into western Canada. In 1890 the Great Falls and Canada narrow gauge railroad was completed from Lethbridge to Great Falls and "the turkey track" took the place of the bull trail.[38]

A STAMPEDE FOLLOWS

FORT STAND OFF, FORT KIPP, OTHER TRADING POSTS EMERGE

J ust as placer gold strikes of the early 1860s sparked a stampede of miners from throughout the country to the newly formed Montana Territory, the striking success of Healy and Hamilton during the winter of 1870 eventually caused a flood of free traders from Fort Benton into the North West Territories. Frontier northern Montana at the time was Blackfeet country; there were few lawmen and a very limited military presence. Across the ill-defined border in northern Blackfoot country, the complete absence of law and order and civil authority encouraged not only "free" trading but also the potential for violent cultural clashes.

Historic strife between Blackfoot and Assiniboine, and their allied Crees, continued. In the spring of 1870, near the Cypress Hills, Peigans defeated a large force of Assiniboine with some 70 Assiniboine slain and the loss of just 1 Peigan. While this one-sided outcome is not known as a "massacre," the imbalanced casualties argue for use of that term. Six months later, about November 1, a large combined Assiniboine-Cree force, vowing revenge, moved toward the Belly River winter camp of Mountain Chief and his South Piegans. What followed was the last great Indian battle on the western Canadian frontier. The Assiniboine-Cree attacked. Beginning with a decided advantage, over the hours that followed, the raid quickly escalated into a major battle as Blood warriors rallied to the defense of the South Piegans. Jerry Potts and the traders at Fort Whoop-Up had returned from Fort Benton for the winter trade, and because of their proximity to the battle, Potts, and

Assiniboine Indians, allies of the Cree, enemies of the Blackfoot. *Overholser Historical Research Center.*

possibly some traders, joined in the battle to aid the Blackfoot. The outcome was a major, although bloody, victory for the Blackfoot, who suffered 42 killed while taking the lives of at least 173 Crees. The Blackfoot winter count calendar recorded the event as "Assinay/itomotsarpi/akaenaskoy," or Assiniboines/when we defeated them/Fort Whoop-Up.[39]

While most traders and bullwhackers moving into Whoop-Up Country were White, they were joined by many Métis, several Mexicans and African Americans. Black men, including Philip Barnes, James Vanlitburg, Henry Mills and William Bond, had long worked for the American Fur Company. Bond became the first whisky trader arrested and jailed after arrival of the North West Mounted Police. Henry Mills, hunter, trapper, Blood tribal member and renowned bullwhacker, was called Six-apekwan or "Black White Man" by the Blackfoot. Colin Thomson, in his study of Black pioneers of Canada, wrote: "In two languages the illiterate Mills coaxed, cajoled and cussed the plodding oxen as few others could." Certainly, unique among the Whoop-Up Black residents was Molly Smith (aka Maclean). Freed from slavery on a Missouri plantation, Molly came up the Missouri River to Fort Benton about 1868. By the mid-1870s, Molly had moved on to the new town

Fort Benton traders in Whoop-Up Country. *Standing left to right:* Mose Solomon, African American Bob Mills and John Largent. *Seated left to right:* Joe Kipp and Henry Kennerly. *Overholser Historical Research Center.*

of Fort Walsh, where she joined the small Black community and worked at a laundry while possibly dabbling in bootlegging by smuggling her whisky in a special leather compartment built into her brassiere.[40]

Leading the initial pack of free traders that followed Healy-Hamilton across the border in the fall of 1870 were Joe Kipp and his partner Charlie Thomas, who built a post with the curious name Fort Standoff. At the time

Joe Kipp, Indian trader between two worlds. Photo by Charles S. Francis. *Author's collection.*

of Joe Kipp's death in 1913, a tribute to him told the story of his two forts, Standoff and Kipp, prepared by the Montana Newspaper Association and published in the *Ronan Pioneer*:

> HOW JOE KIPP INVADED CANADA AND BUILT FORT STAND-OFF; DEFIED HUDSON BAY COMPANY, CHANGING COUNTRY'S HISTORY
>
> Up on the Blackfeet reservation, the old warriors of the tribe, whose recollections of the Buffalo running days are their most cherished possessions, like to seek for the moment forgetfulness of the condition of starvation and suffering, into which many of them have been forced by the Indian Department of the government, in living again those years of their pride and glory on the open prairie. And one of the stories the old men like to tell is how Joe Kipp and Johnny Healy defied the Hudson Bay Company, invaded Canada and built Fort Standoff and Fort Whoop-Up, getting practically all of the trade of the

With the arrival of the Mounted Police, many Montana traders moved their operations south of the border to new towns like Robarre built outside the Blackfeet Reservation. Photo by A.B. Coe. *Author's collection.*

Blackfeet Indians for buffalo robes and putting Fort Benton out of business...as a trading center, besides seriously affecting the Hudson Bay Company's trade with the Blood Indians.

Joe Kipp, who died at Browning in December, 1913, was one of the most picturesque and interesting figures found in the history of Montana from the time of his birth at Fort Union in 1847 until the Buffalo disappeared from the prairies in 1880. The son of James Kipp, the famous factor for the American Fur Company, who came to what is now Montana in 1828, Joseph Kipp was the unquestioned king of the Indian traders during the later years the trader was in his glory. He was the friend and counsel of the Blackfeet, and lived among them till his death. A detailed story of his life would rival the adventures of Kit Carson, but the complete story of Joe Kipp can never be written, for he was close mouthed and uncommunicative concerning himself, resembling in that respect Jim Bridger, so little of whose life is known.

It was in the early 70's that Kipp performed his spectacular coup in the fur trading game, which dealt a serious blow to both the trading posts at Fort Benton and the Hudson Bay Company's trading across the Canadian line, and which caused the dominion government to organize and send west the first contingent of the famous North West Mounted Police, the finest mounted police body that ever existed.

In those days Fort Benton was the only settlement of any importance on the Missouri River west of Sioux City, Ia., and the only one on the plains country of Montana. There was the old fort, built in 1846 and strung along above it in a row, facing the river, were a few log and adobe buildings and shacks, the stores of I.G. Baker & Co., T.C. Power & Brother, Murphy, Neil & Co., J.D. Weatherwax, the Overland hotel and a few combination saloons and gambling halls. But, small as the settlement was, it was the headquarters for all the traders of the country and the center of the great fur trade of the northwest. The steamboats that came up every spring from St Louis with goods for the traders and supplies for Helena and other mountain camps, went back with towering loads of tarpaulin bales of buffalo robes and pelts of beaver, wolf, elk, deer and antelope.

BENTON IS THREATENED

The people at Fort Benton took roll of the traffic to and from the mountain camps and were content with that share of the gold mining business. They were not lured by the enormously rich strikes of Alder Gulch, Last Chance and other places. They felt that in the fur trade, including the important wolfing industry, they had a source of wealth of their own, and it was a line of business they understood and could depend upon. So, they traded with the Indians and with the miners from the mountains, and they prospered.

The best paying portion of their business with the Indians was in the line of winter tanned robes and the wolf pelts that they secured, principally from white wolfers. In those days it was easy for anyone in the winter months to take a few bottles of strychnine and return with several thousands of dollars' worth of wolf pelts. All told there were not more than 200 men engaged in this trading and trapping, and the profits were big for all parties to the bargaining. They were a brave, openhearted, honest set of men, typical of the old western frontier.

But suddenly a cloud appeared on their horizon in 1870 in the form of a United States marshal of the name of Harding [*sic*, Charles D. Hard, deputy marshal 1869–73], with the ultimatum that no more whisky should be shipped into the Indian country, which included Fort Benton and all the territory for hundreds of miles on every side. Hard showed that he meant business by confiscating several stocks of liquor in the town.

INDIANS REFUSE TO TRADE

The Fort Benton Traders realized that their occupation was gone unless they could outwit the marshal, for the Blackfeet, the Gros Ventres and other tribes demanded some whisky along with other trade articles of necessity and luxury, and if the Benton traders could not supply it, all they had to do was to transfer their trade to the Hudson Bay Company across the Canadian line, which concern would give them all the whisky they desired.

The Blackfeet and Gros Ventres chiefs had a council, and finally presented their ultimatum to Joe Kipp, whom they trusted implicitly. He thought over the problem for several days and then sought out his old friend and prospecting partner, Charles Thomas. "Charlie," he said, "I have the scheme. We will go across the Canadian line and build a post where the marshal can't touch us."

"Yes," objected Thomas, "but he'll surely grab us on the trail. It's a hundred and fifty miles to the border and it will be easy to watch us."

But Kipp had a card up his sleeve, and when he had explained all of his plan, he found Thomas entirely willing to try it.

MARSHAL WATCHES KIPP

Marshal Hard was in Fort Benton, watching the traders closely, so one dark night Kipp saddled up and started for Helena, 150 miles away. There he bought 75 cases of high proof alcohol, containing 750 gallons, to be delivered on the Missouri river just below Helena. The goods were bought from Murphy, Neil & Co., who had a store there as well as at Fort Benton. They agreed to re-case the spirits in strong boxes and bind them with wire, but before the job was completed, Hard appeared and set a watch on Kipp. The latter kept his fine black saddle horse at the Overland stables, and many times a day and night Hard would stroll into the stables to see if Kipp's horse was still there. He carefully watched what was put aboard the bull trains going to Fort Benton, and he noted all arrivals from there. It should be explained here that Helena was not considered in the Indian country, and the marshal had no jurisdiction over the sale of liquor there.

About a week after Hard's appearance, Kipp was prepared to move. He got George Scott, a Fort Benton man, to ride Kipp's horse out of town about 1 o'clock in the morning, shortly after Hard had made his last call at the stables before going to bed. Scott was to leave the road well out from the mouth of Prickly Pear Canyon, and cut across to the mouth of Sun river, where he would find Thomas with a wagon outfit.

KIPP FOOLS OFFICER

At daylight the next morning Hard was up and immediately missed the black horse. The stable men would give him no information about it, so he saddled up and hit the trail for Fort Benton, believing Kipp had gone back there after getting a load of liquor out of town in some manner. He was no more than well on his road before Kipp was on the way to the Missouri with his alcohol. There he got the teamsters to make a raft of the 75 cases, piling them two deep, and binding them together firmly with long poles and plenty of rope. On this odd craft, Kipp set out for the mouth of Sun River, at the present site of Great Falls, and his journey was a wet and unpleasant one. As he passed through every little rapid the water swept the top of the raft, and a hundred times a day he had to jump overboard and push it off sand bars.

But at sunset on the third day, he arrived at the mouth of Sun River and found Thomas waiting for him with three four-horse teams and wagons and two teamsters. Scott was also there and agreed to join the outfit as cook. The raft was brought to shore and the men began loading the cases into the wagons. Within an hour a start was made for the north by way of the Indian and Red River cart trail, later known as the Sun River stage road.

HARD CATCHES UP

Three days later, just after crossing the north fork of Milk River, Kipp looked back and saw a lone horseman coming at a fast lope on their trail.

"It's the marshal." said Kipp, briefly, "and right here's where we stand him off."

Hard rode past the first and second wagon without stopping, pulling up at the third, which Kipp was driving at the time. "Well, Joe," he said, with a grin, "I've got you at last. Just turn around and head for Benton."

"Hard, you're just 20 minutes late," replied Kipp. "You should have overtaken us before we crossed the north fork back there."

"Come on," the marshal insisted. "No fooling; this is serious business, so turn your teams around."

"You have no authority here," returned Kipp, "for on this spot we are in Canada. The north fork of Milk river, a mile back, is the line."

Hard was so taken aback that he did not speak for a minute. The international boundary line had not been surveyed and marked. No one knew exactly where the monuments would eventually stand, but it was generally believed that Chief Mountain and the north fork of Milk river were on or very close one way or the other to the forty-ninth degree of north latitude, which constituted the boundary line.

WHERE WAS THE LINE?

Hard finally said: "You have no proof that we are in Canada. I'll take a chance on being south of the line. I arrest you all for having liquor in your possession in the Indian country."

Kipp laughed. "You have no proof that we are not north of the line. We take a chance that we are in Canada, and there are five of us and one of you. Right here we stand you off."

Hard argued and threatened, but his words were wasted, and he no doubt realized the weakness of his position. He suddenly wheeled his horse and rode back on the trail. Later, when the line was surveyed, the spot where he had tried to make the arrest was found to be 300 yards south of the line.

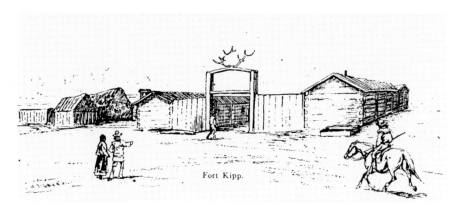

Fort Kipp. Sketch by R.B. Nevitt. *From the* Canadian Illustrated News, *July 2, 1881.*

Kipp went on north to Belly river, and there [in the late summer of 1870] built a trading post which they named Fort Standoff, in commemoration of their experience with the marshal. While the place was being built, the teams were kept busy hauling trade goods and provisions from Fort Benton, and with the coming of the winter the Blackfeet, Bloods and Piegans gathered on the Belly and Old Man's rivers, according to all agreement they had made with Kipp. The country was black with buffalo, and by the time spring came the warehouse held 3,000 fine robes and more than 2,000 small skins, while the trade room was bare of goods.

BUILDING FORT KIPP

...Kipp and Thomas, in the meantime bought a bull train of many wagons, and abandoning Fort Standoff, built Fort Kipp at the junction of the Belly and Old Man's rivers apparently in the summer of 1871. It was not a pretentious place—merely some rough log cabins put up to form three sides of a square, and there was no stockade across the fourth, or south side, facing the river. Differing from the belief of Healy and Hamilton, they rightly had concluded that no fortified post was necessary.

A PROFITABLE WINTER

During the summer and fall great quantities of legitimate trade goods were hauled with bull trains to the two forts from Benton, and plenty of alcohol was brought out by fast four horse teams, despite the watchfulness of the marshal. The three tribes of the Blackfeet, besides the Sarcee [Tsuut'ina Nation] and Gros Ventres [Aaniiih Nation], brought in large numbers of robes, and trade was good....

Following Kipp's arrival at Benton, some Red River [Métis] came in and brought word that the factor of the Hudson Bay company at Fort Calgary had sworn vengeance against the American invader of his territory and was going to clean out Fort Standoff.

The success of the two firms [Healy and Kipp] was so marked that during the ensuing summer other Fort Benton people came north to get a share of the trade, notably J.D. Weatherwax, who built a post just below Fort Kipp. The following winter, 1873–74, all of the posts did a fine trade, something like 9,000 tanned robes going to Benton the following spring.

Luckily for Kipp and Thomas, the Red Coats arrived on the scene [in late 1874] before they had stocked up for the winter

Mule team leaving Fort Benton on the way to Whoop-Up Country. *Overholser Historical Research Center.*

trade. So, ended the contraband trade in the north. [Healy and Hamilton and] Kipp's invasion had been the cause of the westward movement of the North West Mounted Police. The all-powerful Hudson Bay Company had urged their coming, thereby losing their monopoly of the vast fur trading business in the northern country, which had been interrupted by the Americans.

[Kipp and Thomas then] abandoned Fort Kipp and returned to Montana, where they took up a ranch at the place that is now the town of Dupuyer. There they raised cattle for several years and did some freighting between Fort Benton and the mountain towns with their bull train. In 1877 they sold their place to James Grant and dissolved partnership, Kipp…[continued to] trade with the Blackfeet at various points until the last of the bison had vanished.[41]

LIFE AT FORT KIPP

Rare insight into the operation of Fort Kipp came in the *Great Falls Tribune* through an article by W.W. Moses composed as he analyzed the contents of Joe Kipp's account day book. The book documented the customers, reading like a who's who of traders, teamsters, wolfers and others, the famed and the obscure, who roamed the new trading region, the wide scope of trade goods carried at the posts and aspects of life in Whoop-Up Country.

Joseph Kipp Account Book Rare Volume

Record Treasured by John LaMott Contains Names Long Forgotten Entries Made on Old Man's and Belly Rivers Post in 1872–73

Most treasured among the few possessions of John LaMott pioneer trapper and trader of the north Montana Indian country, who married into the Blackfeet tribe and who is now making his home with a daughter at Browning, is an account book containing records of the transactions of Joe Kipp's trading post at the junction of Old Man's river and Belly river in Canada, far north of the Montana boundary, for the years 1872 and 1873.

This book contains entries in the names of traders, trappers and teamsters prominent in the history of the Indian country in northern and north central Montana, many of whom had a large part in the making of the early history of this state and most of whom have long since passed on.

Many of those whose names are inscribed in this book have been forgotten, even to the few remaining old-timers, who were then active in the north country. Among those dealing with Kipp at his far north trading post whose names are still familiar some of whom were known by the present-day residents of northern and central Montana were:

I.G. Baker & Co., Howell Harris, Healy, Hamilton & Co., Charles Ladd, Dan Sample, A.P. Sample, J.D. Weatherwax, John Neubert, Henry Brinkman, Abbott & Scott, C.E. Conrad, R.A. Buckland and George Steele.

MANY OLD-TIMERS

Others who dealt at this trading post, as shown by entries in the old account book, were John Evans, James Flette, Lafayette French, Donald Fisher, William Fargo, William Gladstone, W.A. Giles, James Grey, Jake Graffey, James Hughes, Leon Harrness, John Hyght, George Houk, Thomas Hardwick, Jack the cook for Baker Brothers & Co; Kipp & Weatherwax, Kipp & Thomas, Daniel Keough, H.A. Kanouse, Mr. Madrid [?], John Lacy, John LaMott, Farris Lane, William Martin, Joseph Muffunan, William Clure, George Martin, Had Maine, David Mills, Ed Mitchell, Frank St. Arrioux, Ben Short, A. Steele, William Swank, James Scott, Charles Smith, Charles Thomas, W.A. Thompson, Nelson Veaux, Mighle Welch, Fred Wachter, Tom Whitty, Patrick Coughlin, John Bascan, William Dunette, Jerry Potts, James W. Brown, _____ Deall, James Castedy, J.B. Clarke, H.S. Baker, Joseph Aranna, Joseph Delorme, William Counway, John Duntley, William Preston, Lee Protzman, Sandy Cunningham, John Alexander, John Burl, David Akers, Richard Berry, H.E. Bond, Sol Abbott, Berry & LaMott, Mr. Donnley, Sam Sowers, Bill Bond and Frank Spearson.

...LaMott states that the entries in the account book were largely written by [James W.] "Diamond R" Brown, pioneer, who likewise is still living and located in Browning.

William Martin, one of Kipp's customers at this trading post, was later engaged in operating a woodyard on the Missouri.... It frequently occurred that a steamer would take on wood on the up trip, for which payment would be made on the down trip after collections for freight had been made at Fort Benton. In one instance a captain to whom Martin had sold wood ran past his landing on the down trip with the intention of escaping payment.

In anticipation of such an eventuality, Martin had a horse saddled. This he mounted and, with rifle in hand, rode down the river at a gallop, and finally heading the steamer he called for it to stop. Seeing that it was continuing downstream, Martin fired a shot through the pilot house, whereupon the boat swung in toward shore, the money was placed upon a stake near the water's edge from which Martin retrieved it and then returned to his establishment.

Dick Berry and his brother Ike rode with Quantrill's raiders when they burned Lawrence, Kansas. This illustration by Thomas Nast captures the confusion and panic during Quantrill's lightning-fast guerrilla raids. *From* Harper's Weekly, *1862*.

John LaMott, the present possessor of this early-day record, had followed Kipp into this north country the next year after Kipp first invaded the territory of the Hudson's Bay company. During the latter part of 1872 and the early part of 1873, LaMott, in partnership with Dick Berry, was acting as an independent trader operating on High River, about 75 miles northwest of Kipp's fort. Berry, unknown to LaMott, had been a member of the Quantrill and James gangs [in Missouri]. Their partnership was formed at Fort Whoop-Up, where they secured a stock of liquor and trading goods from J.D. Weatherwax and Scott Wetzel. The firm traded with the Blackfeet, Bloods and Piegans for furs, which they hauled to Fort Benton, selling one lot of buffalo robes at $5 each, and one at $7.40. This partnership lasted for about a year and in 1873, when Berry learned that he had been pardoned, he returned to the states.[42]

Following the arrival of…competing traders, Kipp and Thomas, in 1872, abandoned Fort Standoff and moved to the junction of the Belly and Old Man's rivers, where they built Fort Kipp….

Joe Kipp's later trading post in 1888 near Blackfeet Agency. Photo by Charles S. Francis. *Author's collection.*

Trade Goods and Prices

...According to the entries in Kipp's day book, the wages of laborers and hunters in that far country ranged from $40 to $60 per month, with $50 appearing to have been the customary wage.

Anybody seemed to be able to obtain credit for anything he wanted, and but little money changed hands, the credits being usually in the form of payments for furs, or for goods turned in.

Prices were high for nearly every class of goods, as compared with those of today, with the exception of whiskey, which seems ridiculously low as compared with "bootleg" prices of today [during the years of Prohibition in the United States from 1920 to 1933]. Whiskey, after having been hauled hundreds of miles by wagon from Fort Benton, seems to have had a basic value of $3 per gallon. Still there is a suspicion it may have been "doctored" to a considerable extent and its volume largely increased from its condition upon leaving the distillery.

Just what sort of gambling was carrying on at the Kipp fort, the records do not indicate, but there are numerous charges upon the books for games lost. An entry of September 16, 1872, shows that John Bascan was charged $9 for three games lost, and on the following day he was charged with $2.50 for two games lost, along with $6.25 for five pounds of Navy plug tobacco, and $35 for a bay horse.

Calico seemed to move readily at 25 cents a yard, brown sheeting at 35 cents a yard. Coal oil proved as expensive as whiskey, being sold at the rate of $3 a gallon. Canned fruit was sold at 75 cents a can.

Indicating the class of goods usually purchased by these trappers the following is the ledger account of one of Kipp's customers.

High Priced Tobacco

One plug tobacco 50 cents; one pair shoes $3; three games lost $6; one butcher knife $1.25; one pair pants $9; two bottles mixed whiskey $1; one pair socks $1.50; three cans fruit $2.25; one-half gallon whiskey $1.50; nine yards calico $2.25; four yards cotton

$1; one pair ladies' hose 75 cents; one dozen buttons 25 cents; one spool cotton 25 cents; necklace beads 75 cents; one bottle Jamaica ginger 75 cents; two gallons whiskey $6; four plugs tobacco $3; one pair Gage blankets $7; eight skein thread $1.50; 26 pounds beans $6.50; 30 pounds sugar $10; 25 pounds coffee $10; three pounds table salt $1.70; 16 pounds bacon $4.80; three ounces strychnine $13.50; one dozen yeast powder $5; one pound pepper $1; two sacks flour $26.60; 400 Henry cartridges $16; one paper needles 75 cents; 2½ pounds tobacco $3.25; one gray blanket $3.50; one bar soap 30 cents; one bottle bitters $2; one cup whiskey 50 cents; one can oysters 75 cents; one cow skin $2.50; one pair gloves $3.

John Neubert was charged $90 for board for two men for two months, and $20 for a needle gun, and was given credit for four pair blankets $80, one sack of trade balls $7 and one saddle $10.

Fred Wachter was charged $14 for two gallons of whiskey and $4 for a keg to put it in. He bought two gallons of coal oil at $3 a gallon, 100 pounds of onions for $10, and was charged $10 for a trip to Fort Standoff with two teams of horses.

I.G. Baker & Co.'s store at Fort Benton with bull train ready to leave for Whoop-Up Country. *Overholser Historical Research Center.*

One customer was charged $55 for a Henry rifle, $3 for a hasp and staples, $11 for a pair of boots, and $30 for a white mare, while another was charged 90 cents for three tin cups and 25 cents for a thimble.

As an indication of the prices paid for pelts, Berry & LaMott were credited with $75 for 30 wolf skins; $11.90 for 34 kit fox skins, and $7.50 for six red fox skins.

[After the arrival of the North West Mounted Police] Joseph Kipp…operated several trading posts in Montana, withdrawing from that business only after the complete disappearance of the buffalo. He was one of the most prominent members of the Montana Indian tribes, and was really a leader of the Blackfeet. His father was James Kipp, an old-time bourgeois of the American Fur company and his mother was a Mandan woman, Earth Woman. He was born on the Knife River, in the Dakotas, in 1849, and died at Browning, Mont. in 1913.[43]

REMARKABLE HOWELL HARRIS

HOWELL HARRIS, PIONEER MINER, FREIGHTER, RANCHER OF STATE AND ALBERTA, TELLS OF HIS LIFE, by C.F. Steele, *Tribune* Resident Lethbridge Correspondent

…At the age of 17, Howell Harris went to the Montana placer mines and mined for a few years. In the fall of 1866 he went down the Missouri river to Fort Benton and began freighting. This occupation brought him to Alberta and gave him such a wide acquaintance with many localities of the northwest.

For 25 years Mr. Harris was a resident at Lethbridge and vicinity. His ranch at the forks of Little Bow and Belly rivers was owned by his company until June, 1911, when it was sold and he retired from active business. As a citizen of Lethbridge, he served as a councilman in early years and was also a councilman at Fort Benton for two terms. Mr. Harris was president of the Turf society of Lethbridge, an organization that preceded the present Agricultural society….Fraternally, he was a charter member of the Knights of Pythias and the Independent Order of Odd

Fellows with their lodges at Lethbridge. Mr. Harris was married November 7, 1883, to Emma Babbage of Washington, D.C.

[Howell Harris related his adventures:]
Third Trip to Canada

In September 1871, I was sent by I.G. Baker & Co., to build a trading post near what is now called Slough bottom, at the mouth of the Belly and Old Man rivers, three miles from Fort Kipp, which was built one month before my arrival. We called this post Fort Conrad.

One day, while Mr. [C.E.] Conrad and I were alone in the store about 80 Indians crowded in and tried to take possession, but we eventually succeeded in pacifying them, paid them and got them outside the fort before any damage was done. This fort was burned down by the Indians the following spring and never rebuilt.

I traded there till December, then took some teams loaded with Indian goods and built another post three miles above the present site of High River and traded here until May, 1872.

During that winter the Spitzee cavalry was organized. One day in January a Frenchman named Leon Harneway and Jim McDougall, a cousin of John McDougall, of Edmonton, came to the post after being robbed and pretty roughly handled by Indians. Harneway was shot through the wrist and all the bones were broken. They stayed with us practically all winter. Harneway is now living at St. Albert, near Edmonton.

We were the first ones to winter cattle in Alberta when we were at this post.

I had quite a narrow escape from being shot by an Indian named Starchild. One day the previous fall I caught Starchild clubbing another Indian unmercifully. I interfered, with the result that I had to give Starchild a round thrashing before he would desist. This aroused his enmity and he threatened he would have my scalp hanging on a bush before the season was over. I was on my guard, however, and he did not get his chance till one morning in March. I was outside of the fort looking for Indians with furs to trade. I heard a sharp click behind me and turning around, saw Starchild in the act of putting a Hudson's Bay fuke (gun) under his blanket. I grabbed him by the hair and got hold of his fuke. I led him into the fort and called for Jerry Potts, a Scotch half-breed, who was afterwards one of the best scouts the Mounted Police ever had. Potts wanted to kill him, but I prevailed on him otherwise, gave the Indian a good scare and let him go, telling him at the same time that if he were caught around there again we would have no hesitation in killing him.

Built Several Forts.

Seven years later, while I was at Fort Walsh, this same Starchild killed a police officer named Grayburn. He wasn't arrested till two years afterward. He was given a trial and sent to Stony Mountain penitentiary for life. He contracted consumption and was finally liberated, but died shortly afterward at Whoop-Up.

In the fall [1872] we built another post...near the Blood reserve. We finished the fort about Dec. 10. Mr. [Charles E.] Conrad taking charge, and I started back to Fort Benton Dec. 17 with a bull train. This was the worst trip I ever experienced. It turned intensely cold and a blinding blizzard set in. Every one of our men was badly frozen except Donald Fisher and myself. We traveled 36 hours at a stretch without stopping, and when we got to Teton River in Montana we camped in a coulee which in some measure protected us from the blizzard. This was 50 miles above Fort Benton. Fisher and I turned all the cattle loose and we cooked and looked after the balance of the outfit for 10 days. We had to break up one of our best wagons for fuel. When the storm was over, we started for Benton, but the snow was so deep along the trail we had to follow the river. The river was so winding it took us 17 days to complete the trip. One of our men, a Frenchman named White, died at Benton as a result of this trip, but the rest recovered.

The same night we made camp on the Teton, John Huntsberger and two other men camped just three miles above us. They ran short of matches and Huntsberger burned up a roll of $500 in bills in a vain effort to start a fire. They set out for Choteau the next morning and by good luck came across a party of Indians, who took them in charge and guided them to the town. This was the only thing that saved them. Huntsberger lost both legs and ears and his nose was badly frozen....[44]

FIGURE 1:

Location of Whiskey Posts in Montana, Southern Alberta and Southwestern Saskatchewan

LEGEND

•	whiskey post		△	unknown location
BFA	Blackfeet Agency		C	Canadian posts
M	Montana posts			

Scale 1:1,000,000

CANADIAN POSTS

C1a	Fort Hamilton		C13	Kootenai Brown's		C27	Elbow River Post
C1b	Fort Whoop-Up		C14	Kanouse's		C28	Berry's Post
C2	Pothole Creek		C15	Conrad's Outpost		C29	Livingston's
C3	Captain Jack's Bottom		C16	Grand Forks		C30	French's
C4	Unidentified		C17	Bond's House		C31	Farwell's
C5	Conrad's Post		C18	EdP1-12		C32	Solomon's
C6	Fort Kipp		C19, 20	Spitzee posts		C33	McKay's
C7	Fort Weatherwax		C21	Conrad's?		C34	Willow Creek (lower)
C8	Fort Warren		C22	Campbell's?		C35	Sample's
C9	Slideout		C23	Wachter's?		C36	DkPg-29
C10	Standoff		C24	MacPherson's?		C37	John Joe Springs
C11	Lee's Post		C25	Morgan's		C38	Ed Mahan's Coulee
C12	Farwell's		C26	Berry and Shear's			

Kennedy-Reeves List of "Whisky" Trading Posts in Western Canada. *Overholser Historical Research Center.*

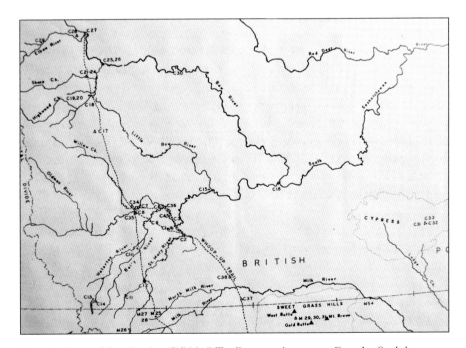

Kennedy-Reeves Map showing "Whisky" Trading posts in western Canada. *Overholser Historical Research Center.*

WHOOP-UP COUNTRY TRADING POSTS

While Fort Hamilton/Whoop-Up was first, and Fort Standoff the second, the startling success of these posts brought a stampede of Fort Benton traders across the Medicine Line to establish many other posts by 1873. Canadian historian Hugh Dempsey, in the pamphlet *Historic Sites of Alberta*, identified about twenty American posts built chiefly by traders from Fort Benton. Dempsey noted that following the transfer of Rupert's Land to Canada in 1869 by the Hudson's Bay Company, until the arrival of the North West Mounted Police in 1874, there was little legal authority in the western plains of Canada. During this time, American traders moved across the border, establishing trading posts as far north as Calgary, and for several years took most of the trade that had gone previously to the HBC. Dempsey observed that while there appears to be a feeling that these posts were set up solely to trade whisky and rob the Indians of horses, furs and other wealth, records prove that larger traders sold mostly the same goods as HBC. But their sale of whisky and repeating rifles did cause considerable havoc among the tribes.

Canadian archaeologists Margaret A. Kennedy and B.O.K. Reeves extensively studied the trading posts of Alberta and reported their results in "An Inventory and Historical Description of Whiskey Posts in South Alberta," which documents forty-three posts. Many records were fragmentary, although as archaeologists, Kennedy and Reeves analyzed a wide variety of sources and recorded the location and descriptions of each post from the best available sources. They also documented associations of each post with persons and events. The result of their study has been an immense step forward in our understanding of posts, locations and activities. The following is a brief compilation of the free trading posts in southern Alberta based on best available information.[45]

FORT HAMILTON/FORT WHOOP-UP. The first trading post built by Fort Benton traders in the North West Territory in January 1870 by John J. Healy and Alfred B. Hamilton at the confluence of St. Mary and Oldman Rivers. This crude post was partially destroyed by fire during the summer of 1870, rebuilt as a more substantial fort in the fall of that year and soon commonly called Fort Whoop-Up. In 1874, when the North West Mounted Police arrived, expecting a battle with hundreds of "whisky traders," David Akers peacefully welcomed the new law enforcers with a dinner, not bullets and booze. Colonel Macleod offered the owners

$10,000, which they refused, saying it had cost $25,000 to build. So, the police moved north to build Fort Macleod.

I.G. BAKER POST. In addition to his "investment" in Fort Hamilton, I.G. Baker operated a branch store "on the Ste. Mary River, north of Hoopup Fort." Exact site is unlocated.

BERRY'S POST. In 1872, Dick Berry started to build near Kanouse's Post on Elbow River, was driven off by Natives and moved on to build a small trading post about twelve miles up the Elbow River. He was later killed by a Blood Indian.

BERRY'S AND SHEAR'S FORT. In February 1875, Mounted Police went after illicit traders in the Highwood country, and made a number of arrests, including Edward L. Smith, from this fort. The rest cleared out, and police found the fort had been burned by Indians.

BOND'S FORT. Trading post of William Bond, half Mexican, half Black, at mouth of coulee in Pine Coulee near present Nanton. In February 1875, Mounted Police arrested William Bond and Harry "Kamoose" Taylor and confiscated their trade robes. (Kamoose means "squaw thief.")

BUFFALO LAKE. Likely not a fixed post, located near a large Métis settlement close to Edmonton.

NEIL CAMPBELL'S FORT. Discovered as an illicit post on Sheep Creek bottom by Mounties during the February 1875 raid. But Campbell continued to operate a legitimate post after being convinced the law had arrived and drowned in 1876 in the Saskatchewan River.

CAPT. JACK'S BOTTOMS (DKPF-54). Captain Jack's Bottoms is located just over six miles downstream from its confluence with Belly River. Although not identified by name, this post may be the Fort Thomas mentioned by Harry Stanford.

CAPT. JACK'S BOTTOMS (DKPF-55). Also located on Capt. Jack's Bottoms, on the east side of Oldman River, about six miles from its confluence with Belly River. The site is close to the old Whoop-Up Trail.

CONRAD'S POST–OLDMAN. Built in 1871 by I.G. Baker & Co. at Belly and Oldman three miles from Fort Kipp on Whiskey Traders or Get-Wood Bottom. Howell Harris called it Fort Conrad. Attacked and burned by Indians in the spring of 1872 and not rebuilt.

CONRAD'S POST–SHEEP CREEK. Located on Sheep Creek by 1873 near where the Fort Macleod Trail crosses the Sheep.

CONRAD'S OUTPOST. One-room post built by Howell Harris and Charles Conrad, operated by Conrad likely in 1871 at the mouth of the Little Bow on the Oldman. Piegans looted it the first summer but did not destroy it.

DKPG-29 BLOOD RESERVE POST. Potential post or cache located on a long, narrow river flat on east side of Belly River directly opposite remains of Fort Kipp. Five depressions may represent trader cache pits.

E.M. TRADING POST. Joel Overholser reported Charles Price Hubbard papers mention of E.M. Trading Post, owned by Canadians Bill Eyl and Jack MaCabe, apparently in 1869, on the South Saskatchewan, twenty miles below the confluence of the Oldman.

ELBOW RIVER POST. Built by H.A. "Fred" Kanouse in 1871 on north side of the Elbow River, about three miles upstream from its confluence with the Bow River, in the present city of Calgary for Hamilton and Healy as an outpost of Fort Whoop-Up. After a siege by Bloods that year, Donald W. Davis, later member of parliament for Alberta and father of G. Rider Davis, took charge and operated it until 1874.

FARWELL'S POST ON ST. MARY. Reported as operated by Abe Farwell on the St. Mary, a well-known stopping place between Benton and Fort Whoop-Up.

FARWELL'S POST ON BATTLE CREEK. In the spring of 1872, Abe Farwell built a trading post along the bank of Battle Creek in the Cypress Hills. The post was situated along a well-used trail and across the creek from Solomon's trading post. Farwell's and Solomon's posts were burned down in June 1873 due to the tragic events of the Cypress Hills Battle between a group of traders and wolfers and North Assiniboine in camp nearby.[46]

FORT KIPP. Built by Joe Kipp and Charles Thomas in the late summer of 1871 near the junction of Belly and Oldman, in an ideal location near a river crossing and within the Blackfoot wintering grounds. James W. Schultz wrote about Fort Quiver (Kipp's Indian name was Raven Quiver): "Fort Quiver consisted of a series of log houses forming three sides of a square. There was a cook room, living room, trade and store rooms. The windows of these were high, so one could not look in through them from the ground.... The trade room of the fort had a high, bullet-proof counter extending clear across it, so high that only the trader's head and shoulders were visible above it. Behind the counter were a few shelves, where tobacco, red and blue cloth, and various other articles were kept."[47]

FORT STANDOFF. Built in the summer of 1870 at junction of Belly and Waterton Rivers by a party that included Joe Kipp and Charles Thomas, assisted by "Dutch Fred" Wachter, W. McLean, Antoine Juneau and "Liver Eating" Johnson. They were stopped at Milk River by U.S. marshal Charles Hard, but Kipp insisted—with the weight of numbers and rifles backing his argument—they were in Canada. Kipp then named his post Standoff in honor of "standing off" the marshal. Wachter took over the post as a residence in 1875. The Mounted Police boarded a small detachment at Standoff, beginning in 1878. New buildings were added in 1885 with barracks, storehouse and stable. In 1890, a new outpost was built and remained with the Mounted Police until 1917.

FORT THOMAS. Unlocated post, possibly on Captain Jack's Bottom close to Fort Kipp. The name may be for Charles Thomas.

FORT WARREN. Two miles downstream from Fort Macleod on Oldman River, H.A. "Fred" Kanouse established the post. In 1873, it was attacked by Kootenai Indians with two Kootenai killed. The Mounted Police used the post as a temporary hospital for an extremely sick man named Brook.

FORT WEATHERWAX. Located on a river bottom on the south side of Oldman River two miles below Fort Macleod, best-known post operated by J.D. Weatherwax. Joseph and Marcella Sheran McFarland built a house very near Fort Weatherwax.

FRENCH'S BLACKFOOT CROSSING. Post of Lafayette French located on the south side of the Bow River, east of a bend. French apparently saved the life of

Chief Crowfoot at High River, set up a trading post at the chief's invitation and continued to operate as a legitimate post after arrival of Mounted Police.

FRENCH'S HIGH RIVER. Located three-quarters of a mile west of the town of High River, French's post is apparently the actual site where French saved Crowfoot's life. Continued to operate as a stopping house as late as 1878.

GRAND FORKS. Tentatively identified as Grand Forks shanties on the east end of Bow Island at the forks of Bow and Oldman Rivers.

HAND HILLS. Unlocated site based on report of an American fort near the Hand Hills.

KENNEDY'S CROSSING. The area at Milk River Crossing close to the international boundary nearly directly south of Fort Walsh became known as Kennedy's Crossing. An unlocated post in that area may have operated before the Boundary Commission showed the location was south of the border, leading to apparent abandonment of the post.

KOOTENAI POST. Located on west side of Lower Waterton Lake, just over half a mile from Waterton Park's entrance gate. About 1873, H.A. "Fred" Kanouse built a post two miles below, later Fort Macleod. This may also have been his "Fort Warren."

LEE'S POST 1ST. Operated near Cardston by W.H. Lee about 1872, also said to have had a later post on the Oldman.

LEE'S POST 2ND. Located at a river crossing on the river bottom east of Pincher Creek, about one-third of a mile from its junction with the Oldman River. It became a popular stopping place after the arrival of the Mounted Police.

LIVINGSTON POST. Sam Livingston built this post twenty miles west of Calgary about 1873, and it operated until 1875.

ED MAHAN'S COULEE. Ed Mahan build a shanty on this coulee located on the Whoop-Up Trail.

MCPHERSON'S POST. Addison McPherson operated this post in 1875 on Sheep River, near present Okotoks, and sold supplies to the Mounted Police at Calgary.

MORGAN'S POST. Mention of this post by Charles Price Hubbard indicates that Morgan had a trading post on Highwood near the Bow River, operated between 1870 and 1872 by Morgan and his partner Bill Eyres. Blackfoot burned Morgan's Post about June 1872.

T.C. POWER POST. W.J. Williams operated this post on commission for T.C. Power, located close to Fort Kipp.

ST. MARY'S SHANTIES. Based on a single recorded observation by George Dawson of shanties at St. Mary's, very close to the international border, originally south of the line and later moved just north.

SAMPLE'S POST. In December 1872, Asa Sample and Howell Harris constructed a trading post near the Spitzee Post on High River. Howell Harris recorded, "I traded there [Fort Conrad] till December [1872], then took some teams with Indian goods and built another post three miles above the present site of High River, and traded here until May, 1873." Sample's Post likely began in association with I.G. Baker through Howell Harris. Asa and Daniel Sample operated this trading post on High River from 1872 until the end of the 1876 trading season. Both Sample brothers were members of the Spitzee Cavalry.

SLIDE-OUT. Group of trading shacks on the Belly between Kipp and Standoff built in 1873. Operated by Mose Solomon, whose assistant Miller was killed by Bloods that year, whereupon a man at the fort suggested they had better "slide-out," giving it its name.

SPITZEE POST—AKERS AND JOHNSON'S. Established on Highwood River near present High River about 1869 by Dave Akers and "Liver Eating" Johnson. The fort was abandoned because of Indian trouble and burned to the ground.[48]

SPITZEE—HARRIS AND SAMPLE'S. Named for Howell Harris and Asa Sample, this post was located three miles above the town of High River and was described as "a long low building surrounded by a stockade eight feet high, 250 feet long and 50 feet wide." Kennedy-Reeves reported, "Spitzee is one of the two most well-preserved whiskey posts known."[49]

TRAIL CREEK. Located at Trail Creek on the Red Deer River, this small post was operated by a Métis family at a Métis settlement.

FRED WACHTER'S. Located very close to Neil Campbell's post on Sheep Creek but otherwise unlocated, this post was the scene in February 1875 of "Dutch Fred" Wachter's killing of Mexican American Joe Aranna, known as "Spanish Joe." In a drunken argument, Dutch Fred crushed Spanish Joe's skull with an iron bar. Two months later, Wachter surrendered to the Mounted Police and was fined and imprisoned. After further investigation, he was acquitted and released.[50]

WILLOW CREEK—LOWER POST. A post possibly operated by Henry Kountz and located on Willow Creek about one mile upstream from its junction with the Oldman and destroyed by Indians.

WILLOW CREEK—UPPER POST. This may have been a trading shanty on the west side of Chain Lakes and today may be in Chain Lake Reservoir.

4

TRADING FOR THEIR LIVES

THE WOLFERS, THE SPITZEE CAVALRY, THE BATTLE OF CYPRESS HILLS

THE WOLFERS

The glamour of buffalo, buffalo hunting and the buffalo trade has long captivated artists and writers. And buffalo robes were the heart of the Indian trade at Fort Benton for decades. Yet, as the great herds diminished by the 1870s, and as cattle began to replace the buffalo and populate the "thousand hills" of Montana Territory, the demand for wolf pelts rose in importance. Wolf fur was gaining favor in the fashion world in the States. Two pelts equaled a buffalo robe in value and became a highly sought commodity. As wolf pelts are lighter and smaller than buffalo robes, a freight wagon could carry many more. Many of the steamboat woodcutters along the Missouri River combined their seasonal wood cutting with wolfing. As demand rose, more and more men began to specialize in wolfing. Unlike robe traders, who left the hunting to the Natives and generally maintained peaceful relations with their trading customers, the "wolfers" did their own hunting and at best maintained a tense coexistence with Natives, upon whose lands they often hunted. While wolfing attracted all sorts of men, it tended to draw the hardest of men. Conflict between wolfers and Indians became increasingly frequent in the new Canadian Dominion North West Territory in the absence of law and order.

The favored method of wolfing was to hunt and kill a buffalo, carve it open and spread a dose of strychnine so that the blood of the dying animal would spread the deadly poison through all parts of the body. Wolves, traveling

Top: Fort Benton levee and Front Street in 1874. *Author's collection.*

Bottom: Iconic landmark Chief Mountain west of the Whoop-Up Trail at the Medicine Line. *Author's collection.*

in packs, would gorge on the carcass and die rapidly in close proximity. The wolfer could then collect and skin the pelts, often from the whole pack of several dozen. Many Indian dogs also fell victim to the poisoned meat, bringing even greater conflict between wolfers and Indians.[51]

THE SPITZEE CAVALRY

By the winter of 1873–74, many American wolfers, joined by traders, organized a band of perhaps one hundred men under the name I-Pit-si, Blackfoot for "High River," commonly called the "Spitzee Cavalry." This gang congregated at Fort Spitzee on the High River, where they organized and passed laws. Among the laws were demands that the trading posts not trade whisky, repeating rifles or ammunition. If the trader refused, he was forced to pay a heavy tax or face the threat of having his post burned to the ground. Irishman John Evans was elected captain and Harry "Kamoose" Taylor secretary of the Spitzee Cavalry. Among the estimated one hundred members, many of them traders, were Sol Abbott, "Bedrock Jim" Bercham, Donald W. Davis, Elijah (Jeff) Devereaux, Charles Duval, Edward Grace, Trevanion Hale, George Hammond, Tom Hardwick, S.A. (Samuel Arthur) Harper, James Hughes, Jimmy McDevitt, Shorty McLaughlin, Bill Preston, Asa and Daniel Sample, Benjamin Short, Charles Smith, "Kamoose" Taylor, S. Vincent and Mike Walsh.[52]

John J. Healy characterized the Spitzee: "There were some traders among them too. I knew all of them. Some of them were friends of mine. There were good men among them, the best there were in Montana, but there were some hard men also among them. They were in desperate shape."[53]

The Spitzee Cavalry began to harass a number of smaller posts. While reports are contradictory, a Spitzee force apparently arrived at Fort Whoop-Up to confront Johnny Healy, notifying him that he would have to quit trading whisky, rifles and ammunition. Expecting them, Healy had seen the cavalry coming and had opened a keg of powder to lay a powder train on the trade store counter. Holding a parley with the intruders while smoking a cigar, fearless Johnny confronted the men. As the argument

Logo for the T.C. Power & Bro. operations. *Overholser Historical Research Center.*

grew increasingly heated, he advanced toward the powder train, finally warning the Spitzee, "If you do not get out of my store, I'll blow you all to blazes, including me." Legend has it that the cavalry, knowing of Johnny's fearless courage, left Fort Whoop-Up and did not return.[54]

The *Helena Weekly Herald* of April 23, 1874, carried an early account of the Spitzee cavalry in action:

> A HEAVY TAX
> The Way They Do Such Things at Whoop-Up.
>
> Last month the trading post of T.C. Power, near Whoop-Up, was subjected to an additional and somewhat irregular tax of about $1,300, and, to obviate the necessity of a future dun for the amount, and any probable disputes which might arise over the justness of the demand, the parties forcibly took possession of and carried off robes and pelts to the full value of the above figures. The tax was levied and collected by a gang of men known as "wolfers," sufficiently numerous to have overpowered any force available at the post. The reason given for this lawless act was, that the agent in charge of the store had been selling breach-loading rifles and fixed ammunition to the Indians. We are credibly informed that the only foundation for this charge was, that a Henry rifle and ammunition had been sold to a white man (and a "wolfer" at that), and that this wolfer had himself "swapped" them off to an Indian for robes. The post is now prepared to defend itself against another similar visitation—which had been threatened.[55]

THE BEST ACCOUNT

Several decades later, in 1907, reporter G.E. Grogan of the *Calgary Herald* interviewed old-timers to compile this account of the legendary gang of wolfers, including a variant on the Healy story:

> The Spitzee Cavalry
>
> "The first mounted corps ever organized in Alberta," said the old men gazing collectively on the stalwart forms of a couple

of Mounted Policemen emerging with a satisfied air from the Alberta hotel, "the first mounted corps ever organized in Alberta was the Spitzee cavalry. It was in the days before the Mounted Police brought the law into the country, and every man was doing what seemed right in his own eyes. The chief business of the little handful of white men living in the country in those days was trading with the Indians, trading whiskey mostly, but 44 rim fire Winchester carbines and cartridges were also greatly coveted by the natives, and also sold to them at a big profit by the traders.

At that time before the extinction of the buffalo, wolves were numerous and their skins were in considerable demand, since the fashion of the sixties demanded that carriage rugs be comprised of them. Consequently, the occupation of trapping these animals for their pelts was a fairly profitable one. But the men engaged in the business naturally had to travel round a good deal in the country of the dreaded Blackfeet, and it was not possible from the nature of their occupation that they could keep together on their trips. Their lives were in constant danger from the Indians, and they resented the trade of carbines and fixed ammunition to these natural enemies of the whites very much.

Accordingly, they organized themselves into an association known as the Spitzee cavalry. Spitzee being the Blackfeet name for High River, with the idea of putting a stop to the sale of those [weapons] to the Indians, by persuasion, if possible, if not then by force. Several men, who up to a quite recent period were living in Alberta, belonged to the Spitzee cavalry, perhaps some are residing here still. I have heard D.W. Davis, the old member, who died the other day in the Yukon, mentioned as one, and old Kamoose B. Taylor, who used to keep a saloon which afterwards blossomed into an hotel in Macleod, as another. Shorty McLauchlin, who used to live on Pine Creek, was another. But no one of them ever cared to talk very much about their connection with the organization, not that anything unlawful was committed by it, as far as ever I heard, but mainly because of the inglorious disbanding."

Down south of Macleod, at the place where the Old Man's river empties into the Belly...flourished in that place a well-known character of those prehistoric days, one Joe Kipp. The

Right: Colonel John Gibbon, commanding U.S. Seventh Infantry at Fort Shaw, 1871–78. *Author's collection*.

Below: Two surviving original 1867 adobe buildings at historic Fort Shaw: *From left*, officers' quarters and regimental commander's quarters. *Author's photo*.

name of the place of abode and business is called after him to this day, Fort Kipp.

When the Spitzee cavalry sent out their warning to all the traders to stop selling rifles and fixed ammunition to the Indians, under pain and penalty of the high displeasure of that body, some thought it best to quit the objectionable practice, but the herald of the society who was sent on an embassy to Joe Kipp, returned with the report that Joe had laughed him to scorn, and persisted in his evil ways.

Accordingly, the regiment was mobilized, and rode, armed to the teeth and vowing vengeance, to the Kipp stronghold. Joe made no opposition to their entrance into his stockade and store, and listened to their threats and harangues with unmoved composure. His sole answer was to twirl a keg with the head shown out from under the counter.

"See that," he demanded, "that's powder." Then he struck a match reached for a box on the shelf, produced a candle, lit it, and stuck it burning in the middle of the keg.

"Now," he went on, "If any of you sons of _____ is inside this store in one minute's time, I'll upset the candle."

The Spitzee cavalry were not like men who wanted the whole side of the house to fall on them before they took a tumble. They recognized the fact that, for some reason or other, Joe did not need their help in running his business and they left him without any tedious ceremony of farewell to his own devices.

This incident inflicted a death blow on the organization, from which it never recovered, and one had to stand in pretty well with an old wolfer before you could get him to talk much about his service in the Spitzee Cavalry. Not long afterwards, the Mounted Police came into the country and accomplished within a few short months the formidable, and what might have almost seemed hopeless task of establishing peace and law and order in all its borders. The fierce and haughty Cree lay down with his hereditary foe, the cruel and blood-thirsty Blackfoot, the trader ceased from whiskey, and the wolfer pursued his calling in peace.[56]

THE CYPRESS HILLS MASSACRE

What began as a skirmish ended as a battle and was declared by Canadian authorities a massacre. In April 1873, a mixed party of about eight American and Canadian traders returning from their winter trade in the North West Territory camped near Fort Benton. The next morning, victims of a nighttime raid, they discovered their horses stolen by unknown Natives. At Fort Benton, the traders sought military assistance from Lieutenant James Bradley and his Seventh Infantry company stationed there, part of the regiment at Fort Shaw under Civil War general John Gibbon. Denied military aid, the traders, led by John H. Evans and Thomas W. Hardwick, departed on a mission to track down and retrieve their stolen horses. Crossing the border into the Cypress Hills, the party tracked the horses to the vicinity of the trading posts of Fort Benton traders Abe Farwell and Mose Solomon and a nearby camp of North Assiniboine. Over the next few hours, a wild and confusing series of events transpired, leaving from twenty to forty Natives and one French Canadian, Ed Legrace, dead. The legend of the Cypress Hills Massacre was born, triggering action by the Canadian government to face at last their law-and-order crisis in the North West Territory.

Assiniboine camp. *Author's collection.*

Many accounts followed with conflicting stories. Among the most complete, presenting the perspective of John C. Duval, a participating trader, is this article that appeared first in the *Fort McLeod Gazette* a decade after the tragic incident and was later published in the *Helena Independent*.

BATTLE OF CYPRESS HILLS
Known as the Cypress Massacre—Causes which Lead to the
Fight—The Battle and Its Results.

Augusta, M.T., Nov. 9.—[Special correspondence of the *Helena Independent*]—I have noticed in your weekly issue of the 4th inst. an article…purporting to be an account of the famous battle of the Cypress Hills. The article is so incorrect, and being a participant in that little affair, I think it will be in order to correct it, so that the public may be benefitted by the only true statement of all the facts relating to that skirmish, and if you think proper to publish it, it will be read eagerly by a great many Montanians. The following is the account as it appeared in the *Fort McLeod Gazette*, and copied by the *Benton Record* of January, 1884, with a few minor corrections by myself.

I am very truly yours,
John C. Duval

THE TRUE ACCOUNT

Near the site of the now dismantled mounted police post, known as Fort Walsh, there occurred ten years ago, (May '73) a desperate battle between some white traders and a band of Indians. The fight has peculiar interest as marking the beginning of an epoch in the northwest history, and one of the reasons for the mounted police expedition in the northwest in '74. Comparatively little is known of this fight and the true account of the causes which led to it, and of the battle itself, have never been published. It is the privilege of the Gazette to give the correct version of the affair for the first time to the public the facts having been obtained from one who participated in the melee, and is a most trustworthy authority.

A brief description of the Cypress…will not be out of place here. It is a deep valley in the country, a deep depression on the face of the earth. High hills encircle it on every side, covered with a thick growth of timber. Various coulees or ravines lead out on to the table-land above, and a small stream finds its crooked way through the bottom. It is indeed a fit abode for savage animals and wild Indians, a forbidding spot, where the wind moans and roars through the mourning cypress trees, and all the surroundings bespeak solitude and desolation, which becomes unpleasantly apparent to any human being who has ever doomed to spend even a short time in this hole, called Cypress....

Such is a nearly accurate sketch, to which all will testify who have been there, of just such a place as one might imagine as the scene of an Indian fight.

In the fall of '72 some Indian traders went to Cypress and established a trading post. They wintered there and built four forts, and traded with the Indians in the vicinity. Early in the spring I.G. Baker's oxen train came out and loaded with the furs that had been traded for during the winter, and two of the forts were then abandoned. The owners leaving for Benton, two other parties remained for the spring trade. About that time a whiteman by the name of Paul Rivers, and two half-breeds went to Long Horse's camp (North Assiniboine) to trade. The Indians were very quarrelsome, and the result was that Rivers was killed and robbed, the two half-breeds barely escaping with their lives. That circumstance effectually put a stop to trade, and the traders, seven in number, had no means of leaving, having sent all their horses to Benton early in the winter, feed being scarce. A short time after Rivers was killed we were visited by a North Assiniboine war party, forty-one in number. They watched around the fort for two days apparently seeking mischief. The partisan chief was persuaded to come in and state his reasons for acting so. He boldly admitted that he came to RUB US OUT.

He was soon convinced that it would be a harder task than he cared to undertake, and he finally left, taking our protestations of friendship to his people. In return they sent two other larger parties on the same errand, and with the same result. Finally, a camp of Salteaux [Ojibwe Aboriginal Canadians], came to the post with the ostensible purpose of trading. Their actions belied them, and on their way in found two of their fore-runners killed and scalped. This had been done by the Blood Indians.

The Salteaux acted badly and accused the traders of "standing in" with the Bloods and forced them to bury the dead Indians and give them a feast to smooth the matter over. They camped there, and traded the next day for ammunition and provisions principally. The second night they were camped there a party of eight men from Fort Benton, M.T., arrived at the trading post—enquiring for a band of eighty head of horses, which had been stolen from Fort Benton four or five days before, and which they had trailed as far as the mouth of Medicine Lodge coulee. The traders told them there were only six horses altogether in the Salteaux camp, they being Dog Indians, i.e., Indians who traveled with dog-trains. Being satisfied that their horses were not in the Salteaux camp, they decided that they would rest one day at the post, and then visit a large Cree camp of four hundred lodges, comprising the whole of the Plains Cree Indians, about twenty miles distant, their idea being to either get their horses, if there, or else help themselves during the night.

While they were resting at the post a young Salteaux mounted a horse belonging to George Hammond, one of the original party of traders, and rode off. George Hammond went to Abe Farwell to consult him as to what was best to do in the matter. Farwell advised him to go to the camp and demand the horse, and if refused, to take horses sufficient to cover the loss, and thereupon [Farwell] took his gun and interpreter, and with Hammond, repaired to the camp, and ASKED FOR AN INTERVIEW with Long Soldier, the head chief. In the meantime, I, knowing the object of their visit, told the Benton party to prepare for trouble, and gave them the reasons why. They, like all prairie men, jumped to a common center and awaited the result of the interview. The party in camp succeeded in seeing the chief, and requested him to send after the Indian who had gone with the horse. This he refused to do. He was then asked for one good horse, or two poor ones to replace the one stolen. This he also refused to do, at the same time calling his visitors cowards and women. When the conversation took this turn the young bucks gathered around and uncovered their rifles and talked very loud and in a threatening tone. The whites, seeing it was useless to make any further attempt to get the horses, turned with the intention of going to the fort. No sooner were their backs turned than two shots were fired by the Indians, the balls whistled close by and warning them that IT WAS TIME TO MAKE HASTE.

They ran and got behind a cut bank on the creek. Abe Farwell skulked off to his fort about five hundred yards distant, and we never saw him again until the fight was over, though George Hammond came to the waiting party through the fire, who in the meantime took a position behind a cut bank immediately in front of the camp. By this time the Indians were shooting quite fast; the whites returned the fire and the fight became general. It was about one o'clock when the fight began. The white men had all lived on the prairie for years and were splendid marksmen. With the cut bank as a breastwork they had full command of the Indians' position and fired few shots but found their mark in the savages. The strength of the contending parties actually in the fight were eleven white men and two half-breeds (two men being left in the fort as a guard) against FORTY LODGES OF INDIANS, which on an average of three bucks to the lodge, would make 130.

At the commencement of the fight the Indians made a charge to carry the position of the whites by storm, but were repulsed with heavy loss by the unerring fire of the white men. Again, they charged almost up to the muzzles of the rifles, but again the storm of bullets drove them back. A third time those plucky warriors returned to almost certain death and again the cool-headed white men hurled them back. No one faltered. Each knew that the lives of the whole party depended upon the conduct of each individual, and to turn their backs was certain death. Desperation doubly armed each one. It was during the three charges that nearly all the slaughter took place among the Indians. After the third charge, the Indians seeing they could not dislodge the whites retreated through their camp to a coulee in the rear, (and left of us) from which they fought for some time, and in order to dislodge them, Tom Hardwick and John Evans mounted their horses and flanked them by gaining a position on the bluffs, from which they poured in A GALLING FIRE and sent them like crows to the timber, from which they in turn tried to flank the flankers, though their move was discovered, and a party started to their support. But instead of mounting their horses and going around a short distance, Ed Grace

[LeGrace], a Canadian of great bravery, rashly started a shorter way through the brush, which was full of Indians, and though he was persuaded against such a course, he persisted, but did not proceed farther than fifty yards when he was shot through the heart, and throwing up his hands exclaimed, "I'm shot," and fell dead. He was the first and only white man killed in the fight.

The Indians who sent the fatal bullet on its way did not live to count the "coup." (Counting coups is the rehearsal by a warrior of exploits in horse stealing, the number of white men and hostile Indians he has killed and scalped, and other deeds of valor.) He was immediately shot by the whites that were behind Grace. This incident threw the Indians into confusion for a time, and at the same time caused Hardwick and Evans on the bluff to notice that something had happened. They watched closely, and saw a sign that made them drop west from their position.

THEY ACTED QUICKLY and waited coming events. They did not wait long, for in a few seconds the bluff was lined with savages, and from their new position they played their fatal shots among the swarthy horde to such good effect that seven of their number fell before they could retreat, which they did sooner than they came. Then our two friends retreated in their turn to the fort, from near which the firing was kept up at long range until sun down. At about 4 o'clock the whites charged the camp and captured two old squaws, whom they treated kindly and afterward released, giving them some provisions and a partial outfit of clothing, etc., to assist them in returning to their people.

At nightfall the whites retreated to the fort. One of the bastions of the fort commanded the Indian camp, and whenever the Indians made an attempt to take down their lodges the men in the fort directed a murderous fire against them, so that they were obliged to leave them standing. They moved off and did not return. The next morning the lodges were taken down and put in a pile with the clothes and other property of the Indians, and burned. The whites knew that the Big Cree camp was close at hand, and that they could put one hundred to one against them in the field. They therefore decided to break up the trading post and return to Benton. Thirty-six Indians were found next morning LYING ON THE GROUND, DEAD.

It is not known how many were wounded, as they were taken away, but it supposed the number was large, as thirty-two are said to have died of their wounds. The white man, Ed. Grace, was buried under the floor of the fort and coal oil poured over the green logs and the fort burned over him, in order that the Indians might not find his body. It was in May, 1873, that this fight took place. It has always been supposed that the Benton party in search of their horses were the cause of the fight, but of course this is wrong, for the Indians had been aching for a fight from the time Rivers was killed until the arrival of the Salteaux at the post, and the stealing of Hammond's horse was the immediate cause of the fight. It must not be supposed that all this could pass unnoticed by either one or the other of the governments. Some "INDIAN RING" SHARPS complained to the Indian department at Washington saying there had been a massacre of Indians in what they supposed was American territory. When it was found that the fight had occurred in the Canadian territory, the United States government laid the matter before the Canadian government on the strength of the statements made by these individuals. [The *Gazette* article then continues with subsequent court action after the arrival of the North West Mounted Police. This will appear in the later chapter on the extradition trial and the Fort Garry prisoners.]

The following is a list of the men that were actually engaged outside the fort in the fight (two remaining inside to guard against surprise) viz.:

OUTSIDE THE FORT.

John Evans, T. [Trevanion] Hale, Thomas Hardwick, Harper, James Hughes, S. Vincent, Ed. Grace, George Hammond, Moses Solomon, Jeff Devereaux, John Duval and two half-breed.

INSIDE THE FORT.

George M. Bell and F. Vogle.[57]

LAW AND ORDER OVER THE HORIZON

Almost one year passed before the press in Montana Territory in the spring of 1874 began anticipating the arrival of Canadian military. The "surveying corps" mentioned below in the *Helena Herald* is the long-needed joint British-American North American Boundary Commission survey (1872–76).

A Military Post at Whoop-Up

We understand that the British Government has become convinced of the necessity therefor, and has ordered the construction of a military post at Whoop-Up, situated at the base of the Rocky Mountains, just above the northern border of Montana. The post is to be completed the present season, and is to be garrisoned by the troops at present doing duty as escort to the surveying corps engaged in locating the line between our own and their country. This will benefit our people in many ways. All supplies for that section must of necessity come from and through our Territory, and the presence of the British troops will have a healthy effect upon the residents and frequenters of that hitherto lawless section where might has so long proclaimed itself right.[58]

THE CONQUERING HEROES ARRIVE

THE GREAT MARCH WEST OF THE NORTH WEST MOUNTED POLICE

A NEED FOR LAW AND ORDER

What began as Healy-Hamilton's crude trading post in January 1870 grew to the major posts of Fort Whoop-Up, Fort Kipp and others. Within another year, this foray led to the stampede of Fort Benton free traders that exploded into about forty-five posts, large and small, fixed and mobile, in the North West Territory. The use of whisky in trading with the Blackfoot, Cree, Assiniboine and Métis grew, and the outbreak of violence among the Indians and traders escalated in the lawless environment as the 1870s progressed. The Hudson Bay Company's loss of the Indian trade, coupled with concern over the lawlessness, led both the company and its allies among the few missionaries in the North West Territory to complain bitterly to the Canadian government in Ottawa.

The Canadian federal government sent observers to gather information and considered suggestions for a corps of mounted riflemen, a series of forts from Manitoba to the Rocky Mountains and a customshouse. Parliament had passed an Act of Prohibition of the sale of whisky to Indians in 1867, yet its provisions remained unenforced, even by the Hudson Bay Company. Finally, in May 1873, Parliament approved the Mounted Police Act, patterned after the Royal Irish Constabulary, which combined aspects of a military and police unit with judicial authority, intended to bring an overall local system of government to the lawless West.

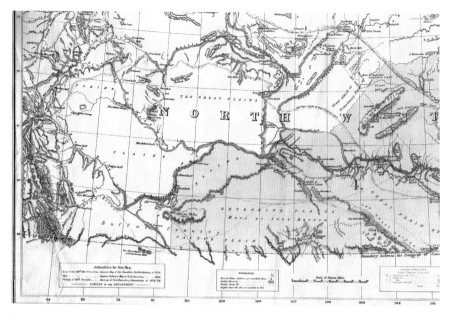

Dominion of Canada Map of North West Territory, 1875. *Author's collection.*

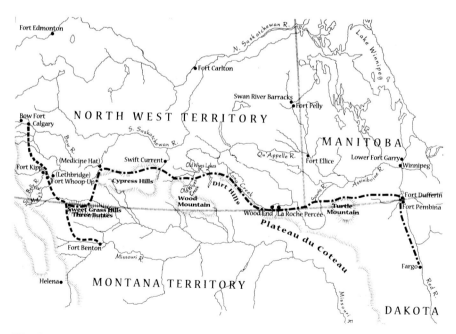

The Great March West. The route of the North West Mounted Police in 1874. *Overholser Historical Research Center.*

"When the Mounted Police Marched Across Western Canada." By F. Van Brussel. *From the* Lethbridge Herald, *July 11, 1935.*

Fort Dufferin, departure post for the Great March West. Sketches in the Northwest. By traveling artist and correspondent Henri Julien. *From the* Canadian Illustrated News, *October 3, 1874.*

The North West Mounted Police were formed and deployed to Fort Dufferin, south of Winnipeg, Manitoba, in early 1874 as they prepared for deployment west. Long glamorously characterized in Canadian literature as "The Great March West," the march, in fact, proved a near great disaster. The Mounted Police, bearing scarlet tunics and riding fine cavalry horses, departed Fort Dufferin on July 8 under command of commissioner Colonel George French, following a trail created two years earlier by the British and U.S. Boundary Commission. The 275-man expedition, organized in six divisions, stretched out a mile and a half with 310 horses, 143 oxen, cattle, 187 Red River carts and wagons and two 9-pounder guns and two mortars. Proceeding at a snail's pace, the expedition left the marked boundary trail on July 29 for a more northerly route to avoid potential contact with Dakota Sioux. In company rode journalist Henri Julien, who was commissioned to write glowing accounts of the triumphant march westward to suppress the evil American whisky traders and bring a glorious era of law and order.

The stage for problems was set by an arrogant leader, Colonel French, who selected "show" horses that were unsuitable for draught work,

A lancer of the North West Mounted Police. "Six Months in the Wilds of the North-West." By Henry Julien. *From the* Canadian Illustrated News, *February 13, 1875.*

Crossing the Dirt Hills: 6th August. "Six Months in the Wilds of the North-West." By Henry Julien. *From the* Canadian Illustrated News, *March 13, 1876.*

Mounted Police losing horses caused this valley to be named Dead Horse Valley. By Henry Julien. *From the* Canadian Illustrated News, *May 8, 1875.*

teamsters with little experience, inadequate commissary provisions and the choice of an uncharted route over dry and rough prairies. The net result was slow progress under unpleasant, difficult conditions—and near disaster.[59]

THE GREAT MARCH WEST

Shortly after the departure from Fort Dufferin, traveling correspondent and artist Henri Julien began his series titled "Six Months in the Wilds of the North-West," which appeared in the *Canadian Illustrated News*:

> We were fairly in for it. Until now it had been all plain sailing—fresh horses, plenty of rest, easy stages, and untired bodies. But from this point, the real difficulties of the expedition became apparent. The very keeping together of so vast a caravan, with so many sluggard animals as oxen, cows and calves, through an untraveled country, was bound to be wearisome. Then there was the ride itself over hundreds of miles, which to the unhardy, was no trifling test of endurance. Add to this that the military regulations had to be severely enforced. No wonder then that the chicken hearted in our band began to make wry faces. It would have been fortunate had they done no more. But this was not to be our luck. At Dufferin thirty or thirty-five of the men deserted the service and took leg bail over the frontier, where, of course, they were safe from pursuit. At the first encampment of ours, two miles from Dufferin, four or five more followed their example. There is no doubt that this had a bad effect on the Force, which, for a few days, was quite manifest, but gradually the distractions of the route effaced it, and we all came to the conclusion that we were well rid of these cowardly fellows, who would have bred trouble at every turn. Later, as I shall tell, the men had reason for complaint in regard to rations and general comfort; but at the beginning, no ground existed therefor. Throughout, the treatment of the men, so far as their officers were concerned, was such as every soldier receives in a campaign.[60]

Evening Guard Parade. "Six Months in the Wilds of the North-West." By Henry Julien. *From the* Canadian Illustrated News, *February 13, 1875.*

Mounted Police Dr. Nevitt in his tent on the March. "Six Months in the Wilds of the North-West." By Henry Julien. *From the* Canadian Illustrated News, *March 13, 1875.*

THREE MONTHS OUT

Struggling on, the Great March at last passed near the Cypress Hills, and Mounted Police officer Captain Cecil E. Denny recorded the expedition's situation:

> We had now been out nearly three months and were nearly 700 miles from Dufferin, but we had far to travel yet, and our stock was daily growing less. What was left were very weak. Our provisions were also getting short, and but for the buffalo we should have been in a bad way. We killed our first buffalo Sept. 1 and a great hunt it was. Nearly every one joined in it. Guns were going off in every direction, and the officers were in the greatest state of excitement. One officer distinguished himself, by his headlong chase, after an old bull with an unloaded revolver. He had forgotten to load it in the excitement. Away he went alongside the bull, pounding away at it, with his revolver slung at the end of a strap, until someone came to his assistance and brought down the game.[61]

IN DESPERATE STRAITS

Finally, nearing the end of their Great March, in the words of editor Joel F. Overholser of the *Fort Benton River Press*, "the party was lost and nearly starving only a few miles from the heavily traveled Whoop-Up Trail and less than 78 miles from Fort Whoop-Up. Snow fell on September 9, so the party turned south to Three Buttes or Sweet Grass Hills," where they went into camp.[62]

Captain Denny continued his narrative as the struggling expedition neared Three Buttes, while their leaders sought salvation in Fort Benton:

> CAMPED AT THREE BUTTES
>
> It was now decided to travel south to the Sweet Grass hills, or Three Buttes, which we could see in the distance, about 80 miles off. We would remain in camp there, while the commissioner [Colonel French] and assistant commissioner [Lieutenant

Above: Mounted Police marching toward the Sweet Grass Hills. "Six Months in the Wilds of the North-West." By Henry Julien. *From the* Canadian Illustrated News, *May 15, 1875.*

Right: N.W. Mounted Police Collage of North West Territory scenes. By Dr. R.B. Nevitt. *From the* Canadian Illustrated News, *July 2, 1881.*

Colonel Macleod] proceeded south to Ft. Benton, Mont, about 100 miles from the Sweet Grass, to communicate with Ottawa and to procure provisions and information. We therefore left Belly river Sept. 15, arriving on Milk river, just north of the West Butte, Sept. 19, after a most dismal journey, many horses scattered all along the trail, unable to travel for want of food. We had one or two snow storms on the road and the weather was cold. On Milk river we had good feed and water. We crossed this stream and camped at the foot of West Butte, near the site of an old boundary survey camp. The boundary line was only half a mile south of us. There was a great scramble for some provisions left in this camp, and one mess was the lucky possessor of a gallon of molasses, a spoonful of which you could not purchase for a fortune, and they were looked upon with envious eyes....

At this place it was decided that D and E troops, with Colonel French should return east. They wintered near Ft. Pelly, on the North Swan river and Swan River barracks was the name given to the place. They were to pick up the wagons and horses left on the road, on their return. We said goodbye to them, and they started on their return journey Sept. 21. Col. French, after leaving Benton, caught them some distance to the eastward.

The remaining three, C B and F [about 150 men], were to remain at the Sweet Grass hills until the return of Colonel Macleod, who would take command of that force, and we should then proceed northeast to do the work we originally came for. Colonel French and Colonel Macleod proceeded to Fort Benton Sept. 22, leaving us in camp with good feed and water, with Captain [William] Winder in command.[63]

Arriving at Fort Benton, Colonels French and Macleod met I.G. Baker's partners, young Confederate veterans Charles E. and William G. Conrad, and quickly set the stage for a powerful relationship between I.G. Baker & Co. and the Mounted Police that would serve both interests well over the next decade—until the arrival of the Canadian Pacific Railroad in the North West Territory in 1883. This brought millions of dollars in business to I.G. Baker & Co. Additionally, the law and order brought by the Mounted Police would bring settlement of the future prairie provinces of Alberta and Saskatchewan, to the great economic benefit of not only Baker but also rival T.C. Power & Bro. Steamboats to Fort Benton brought

Left: Jerry Potts (aka Bear Chief), Fort Benton trader and Metís. Bear Chief became a scout and hero serving with the North West Mounted Police. *Overholser Historical Research Center.*

Below: Baker extended family. *Front row, left to right*: W.G. Conrad, Tom J. Todd, Charles W. Price; *back, left to right*: Charles E. Conrad, I.G. Baker, Dr. D.E. Adams. Todd, Price and Adams all married Conrad sisters.

massive cargo bound for delivery over the Whoop-Up Trail and the later Fort Walsh Trail until the arrival of the railroad.

Meanwhile, on this initial visit of the French and Macleod party to Fort Benton, through Charles Conrad, the Mounted Police learned the lay of the land, including their location in relation to the Whoop-Up Trail, Fort Whoop-Up and the way northwest. In addition, immediate and long-term supply relationships were made with the Conrads, and the "perfect" guide was hired—Jerry Potts, the son of a Scot father and a Blackfoot Blood mother. Captain Denny's narrative continued:

Among the Whisky Traders

We remained in this camp [in Montana Territory] until Sept. 29, when we received word from Ft. Benton from Colonel Macleod to the effect that we were only 60 miles from Ft. Whoop-Up and that we were to move about 17 miles west, when we should strike a well beaten road loading to that place. This trail [the Whoop-Up Trail] was the one used by traders coming up from Ft. Benton to trade with the Indians at the different forts, and was much used. This was most welcome news, as the weather was growing cold and it was not a cheerful prospect to look forward to spending the winter at the Sweet Grass hills. The messenger who brought the news gave us a good account of our country west. He said it was well wooded, with many rivers, and quantities of game. He also disabused our minds of the desperate character of the whisky traders and Indians. He told us the traders were few, most of them having returned to Benton for the winter with their summer loads of fur; that they had also had word of our advent, and we need not expect to catch many of them. The Indians were peaceable, he said, having an abundance of game, and were trading their wares amicably with the whites.

The horses being so few and those left in such poor condition, we had to leave the guns and some wagons at the last camp, sending for them [later]. Our sugar and other necessaries had long since given out, but we had an abundance of antelope and buffalo meat.

While in camp Oct. 1 the first team of traders passed our camp going south with their summer pack of buffalo robes, which they had no doubt traded for whisky. We searched this "outfit" as they called it in the west, but found no liquor. They were objects of great curiosity to us, and we piled them with questions. We camped on Milk river, Oct. 2, about 40 miles from Whoop-Up. At this point we waited until Colonel Macleod came up to us from the south, which he did Oct. 4. The weather had turned cold, and our fires were made with buffalo chips, as the dried dung is called. We hunted continuously, having no trouble in keeping a supply of meat on hand, only having to go just outside the camp for game. The buffalo on one occasion came almost into camp, when one man killed six of them.

Colonel Macleod was accompanied by Mr. [Charles E.] Conrad and Jerry Potts, Blackfoot guide and interpreter, who was engaged at $90 per month, he knowing the country and Indians thoroughly. The half breed guides we brought with us, had returned east with Colonel French. Mr. Conrad was one of the firm of I.G. Baker & company, of Fort Benton, a firm doing a large general business in Montana. Mr. Conrad had been one of the first to build a trading post on Sheep creek, a point about 75 miles north of the present Fort Macleod. He had traded some time extensively in whisky but had not done so for some years previous to our advent. Most of the traders in the North West purchased their goods and sold their furs to this firm, who had the name of being responsible business men. It was composed of I.G. Baker, the head and originator of the firm in Benton many years before, when it was only a stockade trading post, and Charles and William Conrad, who carried on the firm. I.G. Baker resided in St. Louis. This firm did considerable contract work for the different military posts scattered through northern Montana having their headquarters at Benton. At that time Benton was a very small place on the Missouri river, of only a few hundred inhabitants, and these altogether, traders or stockmen. This firm together with that of T.C. Power & Bro., another equally wealthy firm, owned several steamboats that ran to that place from Bismarck, several hundred miles down the river, every summer, bringing in large supplies of goods of all descriptions.

The commissioner while in Benton had contracted with the firm of I.G. Baker & company to furnish us with all supplies needed for a year, by the troops going west. A bull team was on the road loaded with forage and supplies of all kinds, but would not be up for a week or more. These trains were an institution peculiar to the prairies, there being three wagons covered with canvas, to each team, which consisted of 12 yoke of oxen. There were sometimes as many as eight teams of 24 wagons to a train. The wagons often loaded with 7,000 pounds of freight each, or 21,000 pounds to a team. Their rate of travelling was slow, 10 to 15 miles per day, but sure, and they could haul through anything. There was one driver to each team. A night herder and cook, completed the outfit, with generally two or three saddle horses along for herding the cattle at night. The men walked alongside their teams during the day, with their heavy bull whips, which they would crack with the noise of a pistol shot.

All the wagons except what were actually needed to take on the bedding and necessary forage and rations, together with the guns and all the sick horses, were left in my charge with 20 men, at Milk river, to wait until the bull teams came up. They would haul the wagons on from that point until we joined the rest on Old Man's river, at a point to which the guide, Jerry Potts, was to take them. There was a suitable place to establish a permanent camp and build a fort. It is now known as Fort Macleod, the men giving it that name after we had built it, in honor of our commanding officer.

The guide, Potts was a Peigan halfbreed and had made his home in the North West, being well acquainted with the country and all the Indians in it. We could not have gotten a better man, and as proof of his capability in that line, I may say that he was in the employ of the police until his death in 1899, at Fort Macleod, the point to which he first guided us, 39 years ago. The party I had with me numbered 20 men. Some of whom were sick. Only one horse fit for service was left, being my trooper. The weather, while we remained there was cold, but fine, and we enjoyed the rest. Our time was passed principally in shooting antelope or buffalo, which surrounded us in thousands. A few days after we camped here John Glenn, a trader, passed from Benton, loaded with canned provisions, sugar, syrup, and a miscellaneous assortment. He made haste to reach the police when he heard we were in the country, expecting to make a good trade with us, knowing we had been on short allowances for a long time. His expectations were fully realized, as he on

Top: Horses and travois of a Blackfoot wading party. *Bottom*: North West Mounted Police headquarters at Fort Macleod. By Dr. R.B. Nevitt. *From the* Canadian Illustrated News, *July 2, 1881*.

that trip laid the foundation of the tidy fortune he accumulated afterwards. He had been an old miner and trader and knew the country pretty thoroughly.

The men clubbed together and purchased a sack of flour, and a barrel of syrup, which they had to pay a pretty stiff price for. The flour cost $20 a sack, and the syrup $2 per gallon. It was a sight to see the way these unusual luxuries were disposed of. The cooking went on continually until it was all gone.

The bull train arrived in a little over a week later, and our wagons were strung on behind their teams. Some of the men were placed in the wagons, and some on foot, and we once more proceeded slowly on the journey.

We arrived in three days at the St. Mary's river and camped not far from Fort Whoop-Up. It had already been searched by

Mounted Police crossing the Belly River on September 14, 1874. By Henry Julien. *From the Canadian Illustrated News, May 8, 1875.*

Colonel James F. Macleod (*second from right*) with three Mounted Police officers shortly after arrival in the North West Territory. *Overholser Historical Research Center.*

the troops ahead, but nothing had been discovered. On our way into the fort we passed a dead Indian lying near the side of the road. He was an Assiniboine Indian, killed by the Blackfeet, their deadly enemies, and left lying where he fell. He had dried up like a mummy with the hot sun, and was minus the scalp, which the Blackfeet had taken as a trophy.

We found Whoop-Up to be a stockade fort, some hundred yards long and wide, being built in a square, out of solid cottonwood logs, dovetailed together. The buildings on the four sides faced forward around the square. Loop-holes had been cut in the bastions and the fort was the proud possessor of two old fashioned brass field guns, which I doubt could have been used without bursting. Three or four men occupied the fort, being all traders, the owner [manager] of the post D.W. Davis, doing the hospitalities. He took us over the fort and set before us a first class dinner, with fresh vegetables of all sorts raised in his own garden. One of the rooms of the fort was used as a trading store, being full of Indian trading goods composed of blankets, cloth, brass and glass beads, and many other articles of Indian trade. They used coal in their stoves, there being a fine open seam not far from the fort. In fact, all this river from that point down, abounds in coal. Where the Galt coal mine now is at Lethbridge, that point is only seven miles below Fort Whoop-Up.

The men in this fort nearly all had Indian women, having married them according to the custom of the country by purchase, probably for whisky. The squaws were of good feature and physique, and dressed in calico were very respectable in appearance. There were no Indians camped at this place. They had heard of our arrival and had gone out on the plains. The traders had also been notified of our approach, and no doubt had hidden what whisky they had, thus accounting for the non-success of the search made by the troops in passing. We crossed the St. Mary's river a few miles above Whoop-Up, and started on the north side of that river for the main camp on Old Man's river, some 20 miles away....

We crossed the Belly river...the next day, at a place named by the traders, Slide-Out, which name it bears to this day. The Rocky mountains were seemingly quite close to us, looking grand with their white winter covering. They had been in sight ever

North West Mounted Police barracks at Fort Macleod. *Author's collection.*

since we left the Sweet Grass hills, and a grand view we had of them all along from that point. A high range of hills lying to the north, were also in sight for a long time. These are named the Porcupine hills, and lie on the north side of the Old Man's river. We arrived at that river on the third day, and you may be sure we were greeted enthusiastically by all. They were camped on the river bottom, where there was cottonwood timber for miles on both sides of the river.

I was glad to be told that it was the intention to locate here permanently and build a log fort at once. No Indians had come in, but the time had not been wasted. There were two prisoners in camp, one a white man, Taylor by name [Harry "Kamoose" Taylor, "Kamoose" meaning Native woman thief], the other a Spanish negro [William Bond, a Mexican and Black trader] who had been captured the day before up the river, while endeavoring to go south, with several hundred buffalo robes, and a quantity of whisky. The whisky was spilled, and the robes and teams confiscated. The men were fined $250 each and in default, imprisonment for six months. Taylor's fine was paid [by Fort Benton trader John D. Weatherwax], but the negro's was not, and he was confined under guard in a tent and on the fort being built, in the log guard house, from which during the winter he made a bold attempt to escape. He was fired at by the sentry but got away, though wounded. His body was found in the spring by Indians, about 40 miles south [apparently a drowning victim]. Taylor became a respectable citizen, and after being in many different lines of business settled down to hotel keeping in which he still is. He faithfully adhered to his Indian wife, having a large family by her, all of whom he educated well.

It was a relief after all the hardships we had gone through to find that we were at last settled down permanently, with the new country before us to open up, and that the tedious march of 1874, that had taken us over four months to accomplish, was ended.

The weather was cold when we arrived at the Old Man's river, and we camped in tents in the river bottom. At that time there was plenty of cottonwood timber on the bottoms, that could be used for building purposes. As soon as we had a few days' rest, the men were all set to work felling trees and cutting them into 12-foot logs for building. We had such a short time to put up buildings and stables that they were run up in the quickest manner possible. This was by digging long trenches three feet deep, the length of the buildings required then placing 12-foot logs upright side by side in these trenches forming the walls, with logs across for beams. Covering the building with poles, a foot or two of dirt was added. The walls were plastered with clay inside and out. Putting in the windows and doors, the buildings were finished. Very little lumber was brought up in the bull teams with the window sashes. It was just enough for doors, so the ground was our only flooring. These buildings were built in a square with two log buildings on each side They consisted of men's quarters and store room stables on one side and two long buildings facing them, for officers' quarters, orderly room, etc. The buildings were rushed up in quick time, everyone taking a hand, and pretty tough work it was.[64]

MEET "OLD WAXY"—J.D. WEATHERWAX

Fort Benton has been home to many colorful characters over its long history, but few top John David Weatherwax, or, as he was known by his many friends, "Old Waxy." Over six feet tall and bearing a commanding presence, he made and lost fortunes, married and left families in the States and Fort Benton, died early and made his mark at every stop along the frontier from the Belly River to the Judith Basin.

Born in New York in 1840, J.D. married Martha Sanks in Illinois, and by the outbreak of the Civil War, they had two sons. During the war, J.D. made a fortune in cotton and lost it. In 1867, he boarded the steamboat *Agnes* at St. Louis bound "for the mountains." Arriving in Fort Benton, he worked his way into partnership with Winfield Scott Wetzel, and during the 1870s, the firm Wetzel & Weatherwax became famous as an aggressive merchant house competing with the powerful T.C. Power and I.G. Baker firms. By 1871, Weatherwax was trading at his post Fort Weatherwax on the Belly River near Fort Whoop-Up. Canadian missionary John McDougall described meeting Weatherwax shortly before the arrival of the Mounted Police: "'Old Waxy,'…we thought he was well named—cool, calculating, polished,

Mounted Police hearing of trader Edward L. Smith at Neil Campbell's Trading Post in February 1875. By R.B. Nevitt. *From the* Canadian Illustrated News, *July 2, 1881.*

using the finest of English, crafty…[and he bid us farewell, saying,]'Yes, gentlemen, we are glad to see you travelling through our country. We wish you most heartily a bon voyage.'"[65]

On the arrival of the Mounted Police, Reverend McDougall informed Colonel Macleod that Weatherwax, through partners, was operating whisky posts on the Bow River even though Weatherwax was conducting legitimate trade near Fort Macleod. In the words of historian Paul Sharp, "Here was a big catch and Macleod cursed the severe weather and the shortage of horses that prevented an immediate raid on the Bow River posts. But he promised his superior at Fort Pelly that as soon as bull trains brought the illegally purchased robes down the trail to Fort Macleod, he would act."

Before evidence could confirm McDougall's charges, two wagons consigned to Weatherwax were seized, in essence stolen by the Mounted Police. Search yielded no whisky, but 452 bison robes, worth several thousand dollars, were impounded. Colonel Macleod summoned Old Waxy and an alleged partner, Richard Berry. Sharp described Weatherwax's reaction:

> Weatherwax was furious. Vehemently, he denied any connection with the whisky trade, claiming he had sold trading goods to Berry in a legitimate business transaction. "Waxey," as his Benton friends called him, protested that his firm possessed no contraband whisky, though he suspected that the absent Berry might be guilty of an illicit trade with the Indians. Berry, however, could not be found and Macleod was forced to release Weatherwax for the moment.[66]

Colonel Macleod pressed on, and despite a lack of direct evidence, Weatherwax was again summoned and, without trial, imprisoned at Fort Macleod for six months. Old Waxy's many friends in Fort Benton were outraged. Yet for six long months Weatherwax languished in prison. The *Benton Record* and one of its editors, none other than John J. Healy, condemned the unlawful actions of the Mounted Police and Colonel Macleod. The strong Irish Fenian presence in Fort Benton burst to the surface in the pages of the *Record*:

> We knew from experience that wherever the English flag floats, might is right, but we had no idea that the persons and property of American citizens would be trifled with. We surmised, however, that on our frontier, within marching distance of our

troops, almost within hearing distance of our gas-bag-rights of American citizen legislators, the Bulldogs would be properly chained and controlled.[67]

BUSINESS PREVAILS

Yet the Irish rage in Fort Benton was balanced by the strong business community led by I.G. Baker, who was positioned to gain millions of dollars in his firm's new relationship with the Mounted Police. T.C. Power and other business elements also saw the benefits to come by the arrival of law and order in the North West Territory, anticipating that settlers and business would soon follow the arrival of the Mounties. Within a few years, Healy was elected sheriff of the huge Choteau County, and his press attacks were replaced by cooperation in law enforcement. Wise businessman I.G. Baker advised his friends in Ottawa, "The police you stationed north of here are certainly doing a great deal of good in suppressing the whisky trade and controlling the Indians at that point." In the words of Johnny Healy, "In the wake of the police came ranchmen and settlers of every class, and...

Fort Walsh, North West Mounted Police post in the Cypress Hills. *Overholser Historical Research Center.*

Fort Walsh National Historic Site, Saskatchewan, Canada. *Wikimedia Commons Creative Commons Attribution-Share Alike 4.0 International.*

the buffalo moved south into Montana, never to return to the Saskatchewan plains. I went with them."[68]

A Tribute to the Mounties

Just over one decade after the Mounted Police's arrival in the North West Territory, the *Fort Benton River Press* paid tribute to them just as Canadian Louis Riel was leaving exile at St. Peter's Mission in Montana to lead his Cree and Métis people in the Northwest Rebellion of 1885 in the Canadian Red River Valley.

The Mounted Police in the Northwest Territories

The force of mounted police was organized in 1874 for the purpose of suppressing the whisky traffic with the Indians in the Northwest. After the organization the men were mustered

St. Peter's Mission today where Louis Riel taught in the Indian Boys School before leading the 1885 Red River Rebellion. *Author's photo.*

at Emerson, Manitoba, there being only 300 men all told, and this small body of men were expected to keep the Indians in subjection, suppress the whisky traffic, guard an immense territory, free the country of so-called desperadoes, and other duties which would come within their province. They started out, we believe, in May, 1874, for a terrible march over a country absolutely unknown. No traveler had before been over that section. It was intended that the force should be self-supporting, and to further this idea a large number of half-breed carts were put in the service to carry agricultural implements, and in addition to this, two nine-pounder Whitworth guns were taken along—these to drive out the desperadoes from Fort Hamilton or Whoop-Up. The force was supplied with arms condemned by the imperial government and sent to Canada for use of the militia and the commissariat was poorly supplied. However, at the start there was enough spice of adventure in the idea of a march across an unknown country to stir up all the enthusiasm of the men, and the march commenced.

We will not enumerate the difficulties of that terrible time. They were obliged to chain their guides to keep them with the commands; the great quantity of plunder which they were taking along wore the animals out; the dragging of the heavy cannon was a severe tax upon the cavalry horses; the men suffered from hunger.

Nearly six months were consumed in reaching Fort Hamilton on Belly river, where, instead of a gang of desperate men, they met with a courteous and hospitable welcome....An effort was made to purchase the place, but the terms not being satisfactory the disgusted force moved on to Old Man's river and prepared to go into winter quarters. The men set at the labor of building of Fort Macleod, and that after winter had set in.

Troops D and E had early in the march left the command, the former for the post on the Assiniboine [River] known then as Fort Pelly, the latter Fort Edmonton on the Saskatchewan. Troops A, B, C and F wintered at Fort Macleod. The following summer B troop was sent to the Cypress Hills and built Fort Walsh, F troop to Bow river to build Calgary. Detachments from these posts were scattered over the length and breadth of the land at the following places: Wood Mountain, Qu'Appelle, east end of the Cypress Mountains, Fort Kipp, Stand-Off, Milk River near the international boundary line, Carlton and Prince Albert, Fort Pitt and Battleford, on the Saskatchewan, and Fort Ellice, on the Assiniboine.[69]

6

SCRAMBLING FOR ORDER

THE EXTRADITION TRIAL, OLD WAXY AND THE FORT GARRY PRISONERS

The highest priorities for the Mounted Police on their arrival in the North West Territory as they brought law, order and justice were to "conquer" Fort Whoop-Up, shut down the other major forts, suppress the whisky trade and impose justice for the Cypress Hills Massacre. While their arrival and actions through the winter of 1874–75 made significant progress in most of these objectives, the problem of Cypress Hills remained. As they gathered intelligence and identified the participants, they discovered that most of those involved were no longer in the territory. By the spring of 1875, the Mounted Police had formed a plan of action—to seek extradition from Montana for most of the culprits and to imprison any who could be found on Canadian soil. Through the federal government, extradition action began. A fascinating participant in the drama that followed was James T. Stanford, who came west as a Mounted Policeman and, after his discharge, became a major figure in Montana for the rest of his life. Upon Stanford's death in 1926, historian Dan R. Conway, writing in the *Dillon Examiner*, brought his early adventures to light as he entered Whoop-Up Country as a young Mounted Policeman.

The Cypress Hills Massacre

The Late Colonel James T. Stanford Was Clerk at Helena
Investigation of the Crime
    Many lives have entered into the foundation of Montana and none of them is more worthy to be considered in the history of

James T. Stanford, from Mounted Police to Montana entrepreneur and soldier. Photo by Vaughan & Keith, San Francisco. *Author's collection.*

pioneer personalities than the late Colonel James T. Stanford, of Great Falls.

...In the spring of 1875, but a few months following the original organization of the North West Mounted Police, a recruit was sent westward with 21 bundles of uniforms and other supplies from Ottawa, for use of the hard-pressed "Mounties." This youth was James T. Stanford, then 19 years of age. A native of Nova Scotia, Canada, the boy, hearing much of the northwest and craving adventure, had contracted his services to his government, to serve in that new country as yet, to a great extent unexplored....

Coming to the Northwest, as he did, in the turbulent seventies, and being a member of one of the most striking military organizations the West has ever known, the Colonel saw much of real adventure and was witness to many incidents which have found an important place on the pages of Montana history.

THAT CYPRESS HILLS AFFAIR

Most old-timers who were in the territory of Montana in the early seventies, are still able to recall the Cypress Hills massacre, declared by witnesses to be one of the bloodiest and most revolting crimes against the redman in the annals of the West, and an occurrence which caused an almost strained feeling between the Canadian government, within whose domain the incident happened, and the Montana Territorial government. Colonel Stanford was a member of the Canadian delegation sent to the extradition hearing following this massacre, held at Helena in 1875, and his account of the affair...constitutes an interesting historical narrative.

THE EXTRADITION TRIAL

A dozen or more Americans were involved in the incident, which occurred in the summer [May] of 1873 in that range of low-lying hills along Canadian border just north of north-central Montana. It was two years later that five of these men were brought to trial on an extradition proceeding at Helena, an effort being made at this time to have them extradited and taken to Canada for trial before the Mounted Police. At about the same time three others were arrested in Canada and were tried in Winnipeg charged with murder. The extradition proceedings at Helena failed and the prisoners were released amid a wild celebration at the capital. The three tried at Winnipeg were subsequently acquitted because of the fact that their fellows in Montana had been freed. [The five men tried for extradition at Helena were John H. Evans, Trevanion Hale, Samuel Arthur Harper, Thomas W. Hardwick and Elijah John Devereaux. Others implicated in the Cypress Massacre and released: John Duval, George Hammond, Mose Solomon, John McFarland, James Marshall and Charles Smith. The three who were apprehended in Canada and tried at Winnipeg, known as the Fort Garry prisoners, were James Hughes, Philander Vogle/Vogel and George M. Bell.]

Dan Conway continued his story:

SANDERS WAS PROSECUTOR

Lieutenant Colonel J.F. MacLeod, commissioner of the North West Mounted Police, and Major A.G. Irvine, assistant commissioner, headed the party which attended the extradition hearing and represented the Canadian government in the prosecution....Colonel MacLeod, in behalf of his government, employed Colonel Wilbur F. Sanders to assist in the endeavor to secure an extradition of the alleged culprits. Colonel Sanders [the famed vigilante prosecutor and later U.S. senator] conducted a most vigorous prosecution, and as the trial progressed, his case against the prisoners appeared to be most complete. Nevertheless, the men were discharged. Colonel MacLeod pleaded for justice, but without avail, and, incidentally, he himself was arrested in Helena, on a charge of false imprisonment, brought by one of the accused men. This case fell through at once, however.

At this hearing in Helena, one of the most prominent figures was a young man of remarkable physique, tall, muscular, and with the natural military bearing. Colonel James T. Stanford had been a member of the Mounted Police but a few months, and he had been brought across the line to this memorable hearing in the capacity of clerk. He was delegated to make a complete transcript of all the testimony received at Helena, which he did and by long hand. He returned with his commanding officers to the detachment headquarters following the close of the trial.

Many men who were residents of Montana at the time have expressed the opinion that there was no doubt concerning the guilt of these men, but so bitter was the feeling against the Indians in those days, that almost any act against them would have been excused. Feeling in Helena was almost overwhelmingly in favor of the accused men and opposed to the Canadian officials. The night of the acquittal, the streets of Helena were ablaze with bonfires, and according to Colonel Stanford, by midnight Main street and the sidewalks were so thickly strewn with drunken celebrators that passage through was difficult.

This happened in 1875. It is hard to conceive that just fifty years ago conditions and public opinion were so drastically

X. Beidler, U.S. deputy
marshal, frequent
visitor to Fort Benton
and Montana vigilante
hangman. *Author's collection.*

different than in the modern era. In this respect, it is well to
remember that Montana Territory was then but ten years old;
that the territory, and especially the northern part thereof
was very sparsely settled. The redmen were in the majority in
most of the northern communities, and different happenings
and misunderstandings had served to engender this bitter race
hatred. The feeling against the Piegans, Bloods, Crees and other
northern tribes was exceedingly bitter....

COLONEL STANFORD A GUARDSMAN

After severing his connection with the Mounted Police in the late
seventies Colonel Stanford was for a number of years bookkeeper
for the I.G. Baker & Co., firm in Fort Benton. Later he became
connected with the Conrad brothers in the banking business,
and was president of the Conrad Banking company at Great Fall
at the time of his death a couple of weeks ago. Colonel Stanford
was for many years a member of the Montana National Guard,
having enlisted in the early nineties. He was commissioned
a colonel in this organization. During the turbulent days of
1914 in Butte when two labor organizations clashed, and the
city was placed under martial law, the Colonel was appointed

provost marshal and stationed with the Guard at that city for several weeks.…In his passing, Montana loses one more of her illustrious empire builders.[70]

THE EXTRADITION TRIAL

At Fort Benton on June 21, 1875, John H. Evans (twenty-nine), a native of Fort Dodge, Iowa; Trevanion Hale (thirty-five), Glenwood, Iowa; S.A. Harper (twenty-seven), Coshocton, Ohio; Thomas W. Hardwick (thirty-two), Carrollton, Missouri; and Elijah John Devereaux (forty), Maine, were arrested by Deputy Marshals Charles Hard and John "X" Beidler, assisted by the soldiers from the Seventh Infantry, for the killing of Assiniboine Indians at Cypress Mountains in May 1873. The warrant for the arrest of the men was issued at the insistence of special commissioner W.E. Cullen, appointed to investigate the matter. The extradition trial soon followed in Helena, raising intense passions throughout Montana Territory.[71] On July 24, the long trial was over, and the fateful decision came.

DECISION OF THE U.S. COMMISSIONER W.E. CULLEN

Devereaux was released, early in the trial, for lack of evidence showing that he was at the Cypress Hills—even though he had been. After seventeen long, "patient and fair" days of proceedings, the extradition trial ended when Commissioner W.E. Cullen presented his final decision—discharging the prisoners. There would be no extradition to Canada, as reported in the *Helena Herald*:

Discharge of Defendants from Custody.

United States of America—District of Montana Territory—ss. In the matter of the extradition of Thos. Hardwick, et al.

It is perhaps proper for the Commissioner to say that in the investigation of this case, and in the consideration which he has given to the testimony, he has sought to deal impartially with the questions presented. It is due not only to the rights of American citizenship, but to a proper respect for the Government making

Main Street, Fort Macleod. The largest building on the street was the I.G. Baker & Co. store in the center. *Overholser Historical Research Center*

the demand for extradition in this case, and entire good faith on the part of our own Government in observing solemn treaty stipulations, that a patient and fair examination of these cases should be had, and that the Commissioner, or Court, before whom they are heard, should not be biased or influenced by considerations not properly entering into the controversy. That this case has been the subject of considerable newspaper comment, the entire good taste and propriety of which may well be questioned, is a matter to be regretted; but the Commissioner is not sensible that such comments have in any wise influenced the conclusion which he has reached.

[The commissioner then proceeded through three questions that needed to be answered:]

The first question for our consideration is as to the quantum and sufficiency of the proof to be adduced in matters of this kind…."The proof, in all cases under a treaty of extradition, should be not only competent but full and satisfactory that the offense charged has been committed by the fugitive in the foreign jurisdiction—sufficiently so to warrant a conviction in the judgment of the magistrate of the offense with which he is

North West Mounted Police at a small post in the Cypress Hills. *Overholser Historical Research Center.*

charged, if sitting upon the final trial and hearing of the case. No magistrate should order a surrender short of such proof."

…We conclude, then, that the defendants, in a proceeding before a Commissioner for their extradition, are protected by all those safeguards with which they would be surrounded if upon their final trial either before the courts of this country or those of Great Britain, except, perhaps, as to the means or instruments of proof.

Passing now to the consideration of the offence with which these defendants stand charged, let us examine the nature of the offense, and the testimony adduced in support of the complaint made in this case. The complaint contains a number of counts, in some of which these defendants are charged with an assault with intent to commit murder, and in others with having committed the crime of murder upon certain Assiniboine Indians, at Fort Farwell, near the Cypress Mountains, in the northwest territories in the Dominion of Canada, on or about the first day of May, A.D. 1873. Both of these offenses are within the provisions of the treaty, and in both the same degree of malice aforethought, of willful premeditation, is necessary to constitute a crime.

Does the testimony in this case establish the felonious intent of these defendants in the assault which they made upon these Indians? It would seem from the testimony of the prosecution, even, that clearly no design to injure these Indians could have been entertained by these defendants up to within a very short time before they started from Farwell's Fort to go to the Indian camp. The testimony of the principal witness for the prosecution is to the effect that the defendants left their own camp and crossed the river to the side the Indian camp was on, at the solicitation of one [George] Hammond, who is also charged in the complaint, and who had lost a horse which he believed these Indians had stolen; that he urged them to go with him and clean the Indian camp out. The witness further testifies, that desiring to prevent this attack on the Indians, he (the witness) proposed to them that he would go over to the Indian camp and get two horses belonging to the Indians, to hold until they should return Hammond's horse, or until the horse should be found, if he was not stolen; that in pursuance of this proposition he set out and went alone to the Indian camp for this purpose; that shortly after he arrived in the Indian camp, and had made his purpose known to the Indians, he discovered these defendants, with others, crossing the river and taking up a position in the coulee, fifty or sixty yards from the Indian camp, and from which the shooting was subsequently done. The witness swears positively that he did not cross the river in company with these defendants and their party, and accompany them as far as the coulee.

The testimony on the part of the defense is, that the Benton party crossed the river at the instance of Farwell, who desired them to go with him for the purpose of procuring the return of Hammond's horse, or else to procure some of the Indian horses to hold as security for the return of Hammond's horse, (it does not clearly appear which,) and assured them that if they would all go with him there would be no trouble; that acceding to this request, they accompanied Farwell, crossed the river with him and went to a point beyond the coulee, from where the firing afterwards took place, and there stopped, while Farwell went into the camp, which was but a few steps distant.

The testimony on the part of the defense further is, that subsequently and after Farwell had left the Indian camp for the purpose of getting his interpreter, some of the Indians from the camp opened fire on these defendants, who then retreated to the coulee, but a few steps distant, and returned the fire of the Indians, when the killing was done which is complained of in this action. The theory of the defense is in some degree corroborated by Alexis de LaBompard, a witness for the prosecution, who testifies that he saw Mr. Farwell go to the camp of these defendants, saw him start with them to cross the river, and saw him accompany them toward the Indian camp as far as the coulee, where these defendants and their party stopped, while Mr. Farwell proceeded on to the Indian camp alone. It is farther strengthened, in a negative manner, perhaps, by the fact that these defendants knew prior to this time, that their horses, in search of which they had come to Fort Farwell, were not in this camp, and had not been stolen by any of the Indians of this camp; and further, by the fact that some of the members of the Benton party, as it is called, were not engaged in the conflict. Had they been meditating an attack where they were outnumbered three or four to one, it seems likely that they would have mustered to their assistance every member of their party. So far, then, from their going to this camp with a premeditated design to kill these Indians, proof of which is essential to their commitment, the weight of testimony is against the proposition.

The preponderance of testimony is also to the effect that the Indians commenced the firing, though they were doubtless provoked to this by the apparently hostile attitude of the whites. Some of the Indians were intoxicated, and with all their savage fierceness intensified by drink, it would require but little provocation to induce them to commence hostilities. An armed party menacing their camp, no matter for what purpose, was by no means a slight provocation.

If these defendants and their party had gone into the immediate vicinity of this Indian camp, with a premeditated design on their part to kill, and there by their hostile attitude provoked an attack by the Indians, any subsequent killing by them would undoubtedly be murder, and the fact that the Indians first opened fire would be neither justification nor excuse in the eye of the law, nor would it tend to lessen the grade of the offence. But it would seem from the testimony that the most that was contemplated by the defendants and their party in this aggressive movement was to intimidate the Indians, and thus compel them to surrender the horse or horses that Farwell sought to obtain. The conduct of the defendants in thus going to the camp and assuming a hostile attitude is neither to be justified nor excused. It was sheer folly and wantonness on their part, but if they went for no other purpose than that of intimidation, it amounted to no more than an aggravated trespass, and the killing at most was but manslaughter.

The testimony of the principal witness for the prosecution inculpates the defendant Hardwick, together with others of the party whose names are not given, in a second assault upon the Indians a sufficient length of time after the conflict at the coulee had terminated to afford him ample cooling time. If this testimony was corroborated by that, of any other witness it might possibly warrant his commitment for assault with intent to commit murder. But we have seen that this witness was mistaken in his positive assertion that he did not leave his fort and cross the river to the coulee in company with the Benton party. Might he not equally as well be mistaken as to the identity of Thomas Hardwick. He cannot remember who accompanied Hardwick upon this expedition except McFarland; does not know who was present or heard the conversation which he alleges took place between himself and Hardwick at this time, and attributes his lack of attention to details to the confusion which prevailed at this time. Under all the circumstances, it would seem but reasonable and just to give the defendant Hardwick the benefit of the doubt.

The testimony on both sides is of the most conflicting and unsatisfactory character. The witnesses both for the prosecution and defense contradict each other in many important particulars, and not unfrequently contradict themselves. If, in these proceedings, we are to require that full and satisfactory proof which in the language of Judge Nelson would be sufficient to warrant a conviction in the judgment of the magistrate, if sitting upon the final trial and hearing of the case, then the testimony in this case is not sufficient to warrant the further detention of these defendants. It is difficult to believe that an impartial jury, whether in the United States or the Dominion of Canada, would find these defendants guilty upon this testimony of either of the offenses charged against them in this complaint.

I therefore am constrained to discharge the defendants from further custody,

W.E. CULLEN, U.S. Commissioner.[72]

TRIUMPHANT RETURN TO FORT BENTON

The extradition trial was over, the prisoners freed from the threat of extradition to Canada to face murder charges. Helena residents turned out in force that night to celebrate the freedom of these five proclaimed "Kit Carsons" as they prepared to return to Fort Benton.[73]

Proceeding on to Fort Benton, the heroes were greeted in triumph by their hometown. The *Benton Record* reported the big celebration included a mass meeting at Mose Solomon's hall featuring a drawing of the British lion in full flight with an American eagle biting its tail, a rip-roaring speech by Fenian Irishman "General" John J. Donnelly, filled with indignation and triumph, and a celebratory ball until the wee small hours. It is worth noting that General J.J. Donnelly, of the Fenian Army, had just a few years earlier been a leader in Fenian invasions of Canada.

Reception of the Extradition Prisoners

On Thursday evening [July 29] the citizens of Benton appointed a committee to make arrangements for the reception of the late extradition prisoners. The committee entered upon their duties with spirit, and the turn out on Friday proved that they had performed their task to the letter. At 2 o'clock the firing of a cannon notified the people that the procession which was to escort the ex-prisoners into town was about to form. With promptness the procession was brought into line, and a few moments later it moved off in the direction of Discovery Butte, with flags flying, band playing and horses prancing.

A second cannon-shot was the signal for the return of the escort and its charge. The party passed up Third street to the old fort, then down Main street to the Overland Hotel, amid the roar of cannon and cheers of welcome. After several rounds of applause for the prisoners, Commissioner Cullen, and others, the procession dispersed.

At 8 o'clock a meeting was held in the hall of Mr. [Mose] Solomon to deliver an address of welcome, and substantial proof of friendship, to the ex-prisoners. The hall was tastefully decorated. On the American flag were the words, "Home once more," "Didn't extradite," and beneath a drawing of the British Lion in full speed with an American Eagle biting his tail. Mr. John W. Tattan was called to the chair. A deputation was then appointed to escort Messrs. Hale, Evans, Devereaux, Harper and Hardwick to the hall. On their entrance, the feeling of the meeting was evinced in hearty cheers. Col. J.J. Donnelly was introduced, and read the address. Mr. Hale responded in a neat little speech. A purse of money was then handed to Mr. Hale for the benefit of the ex-prisoners. Mr. Hardwick responded in a well delivered oration, although it was his maiden speech. On a call for the Chairman, Mr. Tattan delivered a few appropriate remarks, after which the meeting was dissolved. A Ball followed, and the wee small hours found the boys still slinging the light fantastic.[74]

COL. DONNELLY'S ADDRESS TO THE EXTRADITION PRISONERS

The following address, delivered by Col. J.J. Donnelly at the reception of the extradition prisoners, was unavoidably crowded out of our last issue [of the *Benton Record*].

GENTLEMEN.—The citizens of Benton have imposed upon me the peculiarly agreeable task of expressing their heartfelt sympathy with you in your late trouble, and to welcome you home again among us honorably acquitted and fully vindicated before the law, as you have always been in the estimation of your fellow citizens of this Territory.

On the 21st day of June last a spectacle was presented in this place, which, had it occurred in any Eastern city, town, or hamlet, would have raised a storm of indignation, the thrill of which would have been felt from the Atlantic to the Pacific and from Maine to the Rio Grande. It was that of a peaceful town surrounded and its streets patrolled by armed soldiers, while five of its most respected citizens were seized, chained together, and thrown into a military prison; and this in a town now more than

Powerful Fenian Irish lawyer John J. Donnelly greeted the extradition prisoners on their return to Fort Benton. *Overholser Historical Research Center.*

forty years old, in the history of which not a single instance has occurred in which resistance has been offered to the officers of the law in the discharge of any of their official duties.

In the days of the insurrection, when the nation was struggling for an existence, such scenes were tolerable because they were necessary. But in these days of peace and tranquility the use of an army by civil officers to make arrests where no resistance has been offered, is subversion of the rights of the citizen, obnoxious to the genius of freedom, and a cowardly outrage upon the parties aggrieved. And I desire to say—and I believe I express the unanimous sentiments of the people—that to the officers and soldiers I attach no blame in this affair. They had no choice in the matter, and only acted in obedience to the law which required them to assist the marshal on his demand.

But for the official clothed in a little brief authority, who would thus trample upon the rights of American citizens for the gratification or a Canadian policeman, I have no language sufficiently strong to express my contempt. In you, gentlemen, we recognize the victims of this most unjust, cowardly, and atrocious outrage, and through you we feel the insult offered to every member of this community by the manner of your arrest. Nor were the citizens of Benton slow to enter their protest and to express their indignation, and their voices were re-echoed from the fertile valley of the Gallatin, and reverberated from valley, glen, and hill, and back again to the capital to admonish the venal officials of a most corrupt administration, that trifling with the liberties of American citizens would not be tolerated in this Switzerland of America.

I assure you, gentlemen, that we have watched with anxious care every step in the progress of your trial, for the people of this Territory have been taught to distrust government officials. But fortunately, you found in Commissioner Cullen a just judge, who has by his decision set a stigma upon the acts of all concerned in your arrest, from the British peeler down to the American informer.

And now, gentlemen, for myself, and in the name and on the behalf of the citizens of Benton, I bid you heartily, welcome home.[75]

THE EXTRADITION SALOON

In a final act of vindication and defiance, John H. Evans and Jeff Devereaux, partners in a saloon in the Bloodiest Block in the West on Front Street in Fort Benton, proudly unveiled a new name for their business: the Extradition Saloon. The Extradition was described as one of the most extensive and "very neatly fitted up." A Civil War veteran and town leader, Irishman John Evans assumed leadership of the Benton Fire Brigade and the Home Guards, mobilized during the 1877 Nez Perce War, to deploy to Cow Island during the desperate flight of Chief Joseph's people toward the Canadian border.[76]

RETURN OF WEATHERWAX

Meanwhile, two weeks later, about August 10, Fort Benton merchant John D. Weatherwax finally was released from Canadian prison. Old Waxy had languished in Fort Macleod prison for six months, on questionable charges, without trial and after having thousands of dollars of his goods stolen. He arrived back in Fort Benton on Sunday, August 21, as reported in the *Benton Record*:

Mr. J.D. Weatherwax arrived [at Fort Benton] on Sunday evening from Fort Macleod, where he had undergone a long period of imprisonment. As our readers will remember, Mr. Weatherwax was arrested in British America and thrown into prison at Fort Macleod last February, for alleged complicity in illicit trading with Indians. Though no evidence was submitted that would justify the claim of business association of Mr. Weatherwax and Mr. Berry, the person charged with the offense, as made by the Police, a decree was rendered that a partnership existed and the liability was thrown upon Mr. Weatherwax. We understand the matter will not be allowed to end here, but every possible effort will be made to recover the property now in the hands of the Police.[77]

Old Waxy returned to Fort Benton, a hero among most local residents. He married a young Piegan woman, Mary Bird Tail Woman, and they had at least seven children over the next decade. Many descendants live today on the Blackfeet Reservation. Old Waxy continued his Indian trade at Willow Rounds, staying well south of the Medicine Line. Toward the end of the 1870s, he withdrew from the firm and began ranching and serving as a Choteau County commissioner.

By 1881, fewer buffalo roamed the fertile Judith Basin, and Old Waxy became one of the first ranchers in that broad and fertile basin. He built a log building in the fledgling town of Utica and opened the first store. An old ledger shows one unpaid account for saloon and clothing charges by cowboy artist Charles M. Russell for $36.43. By 1885, genial Old Waxy had extended too much credit to friends, so he lost the store. A few miles above Utica in the Little Belt Mountains, Weatherwax opened a mine in Yogo Gulch. In October 1887, while working his promising claim, he slipped and fell, striking his head and breaking his neck. Old Waxy is buried in the Utica Cemetery.

FORT GARRY PRISONERS

Frustrated by their failure at the extradition trial in Helena, the Mounted Police determined to bring someone to justice for the Cypress Hills "Massacre." Three men were located, still on Canadian soil, who had been present in the Cypress Hills during the battle in May 1873. In September 1875, James Hughes, Philander Vogle/Vogel and George M. Bell were arrested and incarcerated at Fort Garry near Winnipeg, Manitoba. The three were charged with the murder of several Indian men, women and children. The *Benton Record* set the scene for the trial of the Fort Garry prisoners:

THE FORT GARRY PRISONERS

If the evidence presented at Helena was not sufficient to cause an unbiased juror to grant a committal, surely the testimony obtained at Fort McLeod could not justify an examining magistrate in committing the members of the accused, when only two out of the many prosecuting witnesses were present to testify, and those two, Farwell and his ex-interpreter LaBompard. Farwell's evidence at Helena was neither truthful nor of sufficient strength to convict the accused of any crime. LaBompard could not recognize anybody connected with the affair.

Upon this same evidence Vogel and Hughes have been hustled off to Fort Garry to be held and duly tried; and it is but natural to infer from the preliminary proceedings, in which the evidence of the defense was excluded, that the matter is so arranged that no witnesses can be called by the accused men at their trial. This plan must succeed, if not frustrated by our Government. The witnesses which these men would call upon are in Montana, many of them in Benton. They dare not go to Fort Garry for fear they themselves may be arrested on the same charge. It is therefore the duty of our Government to see that these prisoners now confined at Fort Garry receive a fair trial, and that any witnesses upon whom they may call are subpoenaed in a proper manner, and that they go and return under protection of the United States flag.

One of the prisoners, Vogel, was employed at Cypress Mountains at the time of the fight; the other, Hughes, belonged to the Benton party. Vogel, it was alleged at the examination at Helena, was riding a horse that had belonged to the Indians with whom the white men fought. Upon this, we presume, Vogel is held. But there is evidence here at Benton to show that, at the time, Vogel's feet were frozen, that he was therefore unable to walk, and desired to go towards Whoop-Up with the white men, after the fight, but had no horse until a half-breed gave him the one in question to perform his journey. We know that there is evidence enough to prove this, and it seems impossible that the man should be allowed to suffer for want of this testimony. Hughes was one of the Benton party, and that is all that need be said concerning him in connection with this case. There was no evidence to convict him at Helena, yet the people of this Territory, the people of these United States, are insultingly told that the evidence upon which a conscientious American Juror refused to commit, was more than sufficient to convict an American in Canada. That is the sum and substance of it.[78]

Through Montana territorial governor Benjamin Potts, the Canadian government attempted to entice the Fort Benton men into returning to Winnipeg for the trial of the Fort Garry prisoners in October. Since the men were convinced that the Canadian government would throw them into prison once they crossed the border, the potential witnesses refused to cooperate. Still bitter over the extradition trial, Trevanion Hale explained their refusal:

Correspondence Between Governor Potts and Trevanion Hale
Executive Department,
Helena, M.T., Sept. 22, 1875.

To T. Hale, Fort Benton, Montana,
Sir: -- Vogle, Bell and Hughes, citizens of Montana, have been arrested by the Canadian authorities and are held for trial at Fort Garry, October fifteenth, for the murder of certain Indians at Cypress Hill in 1873. The above named parties desire your attendance as a witness in their behalf at Fort Garry 15th proximo. Also, the attendance as witnesses of Jeff Devereaux, John Deval, Joseph Carr, John Joe, and George Powell. You will please notify the said parties of the place and time of trial and of the request of Vogle, Bell and Hughes. Very Truly, B.F. Potts, Governor of Montana.

To Hon. B.F. Potts, Gov. of Montana, Helena, M.T.
SIR: —I have the honor to acknowledge the receipt of your communication of the 22nd inst, relative to my attendance as a witness at the trial of Vogle, Bell, and Hughes, at Fort Garry,

B.A., on the 15ᵗʰ of October next. As directed, I have notified the parties mentioned by you, except Carr, who is at present at or near Fort McLeod, B.A.

It would be an act of injustice to ourselves and to the men imprisoned at Fort Garry, to allow this bare acknowledgement to escape without an explanation of the cause of our inability to proceed to Fort Garry as witnesses, and of the nature of the evidence of which the prisoners are consequentially deprived. At the time of the fight, Vogle was in the employ of Moses Solomon, and was a cripple. His feet had been frozen, and he could not walk without the aid of crutches. He was not in any way connected with the fight.

After the fight, Vogle desired to proceed to Whoop-Up with some of our party, but he had no means of transportation. On learning this, a half-breed gave his horse, which it seems belonged to the camp of Indians that fired on us. Of this, however, Vogle was ignorant. Immediately preceding the fight, Bell was in the employ of Solomon as night watchman. In consequence of the hostility of the Indians and of their repeated threats to clean out the white men, this precaution became necessary, and on our arrival at Solomon's fort, Bell was performing that duty. On the day of the fight, as far as we know, Bell was in Solomon's fort. We are positive that he was not in any way engaged in the fight. Hughes was the only one of the three men that belonged to our party, which was known during the examination at Helena, M.T., as the Benton party. At the time the fighting occurred Hughes was not with us, he was on the other side of the river near the Forts of Farwell and Solomon. During the fight Hughes did not connect with us, nor at any time until all was over. He could not have engaged in the fight without our knowledge.

Without going into details of the evidence, the above brief summary of the same which we are willing to tender, will enable your Excellency to perceive the necessity of immediate steps being taken by the United States authorities to stay the trial, and to procure the valuable testimony which is at the command of the United States Government, lest these men, its own citizens, who are truly innocent, should in the absence of this evidence be declared guilty on the perjured and paid testimony of a paid informer. The United States Commissioner, W.E. Cullen, can testify as to the evidence produced by the Canadian Government, assisted by the officials of our Government at Helena. He will testify that no evidence was adduced that in any manner could connect the men imprisoned at Fort Garry with our actions at Cypress Hill save what has just been presented to you in the above summary.

Those who have been notified through your communication as being required as witnesses, are willing to proceed to Fort Garry. But no one could possibly imagine that we would go there without proper protection. The examination at Helena, its expense and consequent disaster to our business, has left us without the means of proceeding on a journey such as the one in question, even had we the protection, going and coming, of the United States. And without that protection, it could not be reasonably expected that we would leave our homes already shattered through the action of the Canadian government against us, perhaps never to return to them. Perhaps on our arrival on British soil we may be arrested by the same officers, chained in the same den which holds the men whom we can prove innocent of the charges preferred against them by the Canadian authorities. In short, your Excellency, the witnesses who can prove the innocence of Vogle, Bell, and Hughes are at this place unable to proceed to the place of trial, and awaiting the protection and pecuniary support of the U.S. Government to proceed to and return from the trial of their fellow citizens.

Very respectfully, your obedient servant.

TREVANION HALE[79]

In early October, letters came to John Evans from the three prisoners awaiting trial at Fort Garry. From the *Benton Record* of October 9:

Mr. J.H. Evans is in receipt of letters from the Fort Garry prisoners. They unite in beseeching the assistance of their friends in Montana, in their hour of misery. They are in a very precarious condition, just now and we judge from their words that they are fully cognizant of that fact. The notorious Farwell, the model witness, whose perjured lips move glibly in the self-imposed, paid task of convicting innocent men, by his false tales, and the long haired half-breed LaBompard, who a few months ago was unable to identify any of the accused parties with the charge preferred by the Canadian authorities, are the main witnesses for the prosecution....

If the Canadian authorities are really anxious to promote the ends of justice, they should turn the tables. Examine Vogle, Bell and Hughes as witnesses, and put Farwell where in the course of events he will undoubtedly be placed, in the dock. Those men can prove that Farwell is a notorious liar that he had been a whisky trader in the Northwest British possessions for many years, and that he was the cause, the originator, the prime mover in the difficulty which ensued between the Indians and the white men at the time in question....

Mr. Hughes, in his letter says: "Bell had an examination here and was committed to prison on a charge of murder. Mr. Taylor, the United States Consul, has been attending to us since we have been here, but though he is sincere in his friendship, he cannot perform impossibilities. So far, we have found him to be a thorough gentleman and a credit to the nation he represents."

We have reason to know that our Consul at Fort Garry is all that Mr. Hughes represents him, and that he will not hesitate to perform his duty in guarding the lives, and liberties of the American citizens now prisoners at that place.[80]

The Trial Opens

On October 11, the trial of the Fort Garry prisoners opened at the Court of Queen's Bench in Winnipeg, Manitoba. On the second day of the trial, charges were broadened to include Thomas Hardwick, Trevanion Hale, John Evans, Philander Vogle, Arthur Harper, Jeff Devereaux, J. Duval, George M. Bell, George Hammond, Mose Solomon, John McFarland, James Hughes, James Marshall and Charles Smith, all men freed by Commissioner Cullen at the end of the extradition trial in Helena. The specific charges were that on May 25, 1873, the said parties did, while at the Cypress Hills, feloniously, willfully and of malice aforethought murder a female Indian of the North Assiniboine tribe. The second indictment against the parties was for the murder of a male Indian of said tribe named Little Soldier—the murder at the same time at Cypress

Hills. And the third indictment was for the murder at the same time and place of an Indian named Manito-co-pah-oh-tis (a male Native of the North Assiniboine tribe).[81]

A LONG DELAY

While the Court of Queen's Bench trial began in mid-October 1875, long delays were incurred until June 1876, when proceedings finally resumed. Meanwhile, further attempts were made to entice the extradition trial men to return to Winnipeg as witnesses. Meanwhile, prisoners Bell, Hughes and Vogel/Vogle remained in Canadian prison. The press in Helena and Fort Benton continued to urge their release. On June 1, John Evans pleaded for Montanans to donate funds for the defense of the prisoners.

The trial finally resumed on June 19, 1876, in the Court of Queen's Bench in Winnipeg. More trouble followed in empaneling a jury, but the trial at last began. Over the next days, the evidence of Abe Farwell, LaBompard and Mrs. Farwell was presented. The extradition trial men refused to return to British America, although John H. Evans and Trevanion Hale of Fort Benton provided testimony through affidavit. The case presented by the Canadian government was even weaker than at the extradition trial, and the new trial was over in just four days. On June 22, the trial of the Fort Garry prisoners ended, as reported in the *Manitoba Free Press*:

> We thus have
>
> After His Lordship explained to the jury that as the prisoners had pleaded separately, they might find one guilty and acquit the others, they retired and after a short deliberation returned a verdict of "not guilty."
>
> As there were still two indictments against the prisoners, one for the murder of an Indian woman and the other for the killing of an unknown Indian, Mr. Cornish said he would telegraph to the Department of Justice for instructions.
>
> On motion of Mr. Cornish they were released upon their own recognizances to appear when called upon.[82]

Three weeks later, news of the not guilty verdict reached Fort Benton in a letter to John Evans. Bell, Hughes and Vogel/Vogle still faced two remaining charges but were released to return to Fort Benton. They quickly departed Winnipeg by stage to Bismarck and there boarded the steamboat *Key West* to come up the Missouri River to arrive at Fort Benton on July 18 after their long ordeal.

Almost six more years would pass before the Court of Queen's Bench in Winnipeg finally closed out the remaining indictments against the Cypress Hills men. The *Benton Record* celebrated this belated "vindication":

A FINAL VINDICATION

The community, and indeed the people of the Territory at large will be pleased to read the appended certificate from the Court of Queen's Bench, Manitoba, in the famous extradition cases. The *nolle prosequi* has ended the matter, and after 7 years of patient waiting, the men whose names were written down to answer the charge of murder have been completely vindicated by the Canadian authorities. Great credit is due to John H. Evans, of Benton, for securing the *nolle prosequi* and to the American Consul, Mr. J.W. Taylor, at Winnipeg, for his invaluable aid to his countrymen.

The history of the affair is familiar to all old timers in Montana, and has from time to time been told in our columns. We congratulate the parties interested upon the final termination of the case and award full praise to Mr. Evans for the patriotic interest he has shown in removing a black spot from his own and his fellow countrymen's names.[83]

THE FATE OF FARWELL

After his "failed" testimony in both the extradition and Fort Garry prisoners trials, former whisky trader Abe Farwell returned to Montana Territory and tried to resettle at Fort Benton. Faced with bitter and vindictive enemies, Farwell fled to southern Montana to live a short and miserable life. He committed suicide near Park City. The *River Press* reported the sad end for Abel Farwell in May 1886.

Death of Abel Farwell

The *Billings Gazette* of the 10th inst. It contains an account of the death of Abel Farwell. It seems that he resided somewhere on Clark's Fork and had sent a Mexican to Park City for two bottles of whisky. He drank one bottle and told his companion that it contained poison, which, however, did not deter him from finishing the other bottle the same day. A messenger was sent to Park City for remedies, but he died before the messenger returned. The body was taken to Billings and an autopsy held. The verdict was that he died from congestion of the brain, the result of chronic alcoholism.

Abel Farwell leaves no friends in this section of Montana, where he is well, but unfavorably known. It was through his lying representations and turning state's evidence that caused the arrest of a number of reputable citizens of Fort Benton for alleged complicity in the so called "Cypress Hills massacre," in 1873, we believe, although the arrest did not take place until the spring of 1875, when a company of U.S. cavalry surrounded the town and the U.S. marshal was enabled to secure his prisoners, who were bound and taken to Helena, tried and discharged, evidence not being sufficient to warrant their extradition. It was during the trial that Farwell made himself famous by his lying statement to secure the conviction of his former friends. A short time after the trial he left this part of the country and went down on the Yellowstone, where he has lived ever since.[84]

REMEMBERING SHARED BONDS

TALES OF WHOOP-UP COUNTRY

The wagon trail that began in 1870, following long-worn Indian trails from Canada to Fort Benton, saw heavy use throughout the Whoop-Up years until the arrival of the Mounted Police in the fall of 1874. The trail then extended on to Fort Macleod and other settlements as they emerged in the North West Territory. Use of the trail continued and accelerated over the next decade with supplies for the Mounted Police and the settlers and settlements that moved into the North West Territory with law and order. All things Mounted Police, from new recruits to supplies, even payroll, came up the Missouri by steamboat and on to the trail. Most supplies for the new farms, ranches and settlements came up by steamboat for overland freighting up the Whoop-Up Trail until the Canadian Pacific Railroad arrived in 1883. Many return wagons brought coal from the new Nicholas Sheran mines near Fort Whoop-Up in addition to robes and other trade. More than a dozen years of heavy use left a well-worn Whoop-Up Trail. Charles Schafft, an early pioneer and a most uncommon visitor, captured the colorful essence of Whoop-Up Country well when he wrote in the *Benton Record*:

> A few years ago when a man suddenly and mysteriously disappeared from his accustomed haunts, and the inquiry was passed around, "What has become of him?" the answer and conclusion arrived at in some instances was, that he had gone

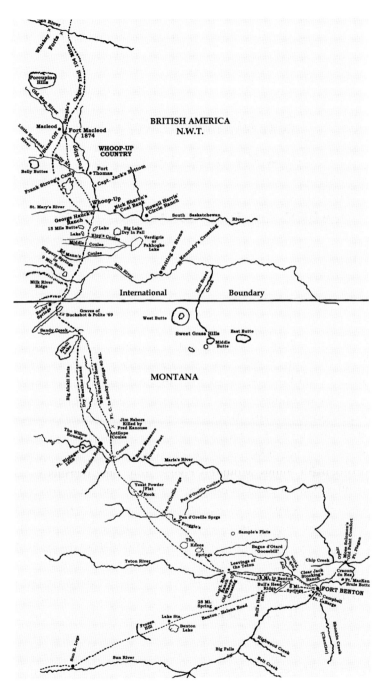

Harry Stanford's Whoop-Up map. *Overholser Historical Research Center.*

I.G. Baker & Co. store at Fort Macleod did booming business until arrival of the Canadian Pacific Railroad. *Overholser Historical Research Center.*

Grand I.G. Baker & Co. store in Calgary, a symbol of the powerful role played by this company in the North West Territory until the arrival of the Canadian Pacific Railroad. *Overholser Historical Research Center.*

across the line to "Whoop-Up"; and the very mention of that place would cause the imagination to picture forth red-handed desperadoes performing bloody deeds, and defying the laws of civilization in a secluded wilderness made almost inaccessible to the ordinary mortal, owing to the dangers reported to be besetting the trails leading in that direction.[85]

TRADING POSTS AFTER THE ARRIVAL OF THE MOUNTIES

While most of the smaller American trading posts closed down with the arrival of the Mounted Police, others began to emerge, sanctioned by the Mounties. I.G. Baker & Co. built trading posts at Fort Macleod and Calgary as that frontier town began to build. A trail from Fort Benton opened into the Cypress Hills known as the Fort Walsh Trail, and in October 1875, Henry A. Kennerly went up the trail to build a trading post for T.C. Power at the new Mounted Police post at Fort Walsh. The Riplinger Trail from Sun River Crossing, used by Healy and Hamilton on their fateful expedition across the Medicine Line in early 1870, continued to have some use, with stops at the Blackfeet Agency along the way.[86]

The *Helena Herald* carried *Benton Record* news waxing optimistic about the future trade in Whoop-Up Country and the continuing bison robe trade in the fall of 1875:

> We condense the following items from our Fort Macleod correspondent:
>
> The prospects of the fur trade are favorably increasing. Buffalo plenty and Indians numerous. Building is still in order. Baker & Co. are building on Bow River; [T.C.] Power & Bro. have built at Macleod and are now building a post on Bow River. The police fort will not be constructed this fall. Mr. T.J. Bogy has arrived here to manage the trading business of Power & Bro. A.B. Keeler still assists W. [*sic*, Charles E.] Conrad in Baker's establishment. A teamster in the employ of Power & Bro. was accidentally drowned a few days ago in the creek which surrounds the Police fort; quite a town is being established here; over twenty houses have been built lately and are inhabited by white people. Large quantities of coal are being shipped to Montana.

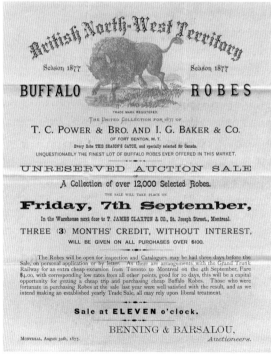

Above: Steamboat *Rose Bud* at Judith Landing on the Missouri River with Mounted Police passengers in pith helmets and cargo bound for the North West Territory. *U.S. National Archives and Records Administration.*

Left: T.C. Power & Bro and I.G. Baker & Co.'s 1877 auction in Montreal of twelve thousand "Selected Robes" from the British North-West Territory. *Author's photo.*

Burnett's train rolled out for Cypress loaded with 30,000 pounds of merchandise for T.C. Power & Bro. on Thursday.

Twenty-five tons of coal is being forwarded from British America to T.C. Power & Bro.

J.D. Weatherwax has gone to his post at Willow Rounds. [Trading well south of the border.]

John W. Power arrived from Fort Macleod on Sunday.[87]

TALES OF WHOOP-UP COUNTRY

Many, many pioneers had memories of the Whoop-Up Trail and the amazing five years when so many were "whoopin-em up" on the trail and north of the Medicine Line—perhaps no trail in Montana has more stories featuring the colorful years. It was a short period filled with many exciting, intense memories, shared by many pioneers.

In the sampling of reminiscences that follow, no traveler presented a more vibrant and detailed portrait of the Whoop-Up Trail and its times than Charles Schafft. Born in Russia in 1838, Charles Schafft came to New York in 1849 to join his father. After Schafft enlisted in the army and survived two shipwrecks, his Third Artillery Regiment finally made it to San Diego in 1854. Serving until discharged four years later, he met Lieutenant John Mullan, who promised to hire Schafft as part of his road building expedition designed to link Fort Benton, on the Missouri River, to Fort Walla Walla, on the Columbia River. Hired as a commissary herder to drive the beef cattle going on the Mullan Military Wagon Road Expedition, Schafft served until winter quarters were established in December 1859 at Camp Jordan near Regis Borgia. Leaving the expedition, Schafft had a series of adventures before rejoining Mullan's expedition doing further road work in 1861. In January 1862, Schafft set out for the Deer Lodge valley, where in sub-zero temperatures, he broke through ice and badly froze his feet up to his ankles before struggling into a soldiers' camp. In March, both of Schafft's legs were amputated within six inches of the knee joints. Remarkably, overcoming his immense handicap, Charles Schafft continued his adventures in new Montana Territory, serving as Missoula County's first clerk and recorder and in various clerical and accounting positions at the Flathead Indian Agency. At a time of turmoil at the agency in 1874, Schafft described his actions:[88]

I skipped the country and went across the "Line" to Whoop Up, supposed to be then a resort of the most desperate characters escaped from the United States. I saw some dead bodies there, but the place was not as bad as represented. I was there partly in charge of the principal Fort [Whoop-Up], when Col. McLeod and his 300 mounted Police arrived from Fort Garry, to subdue the outlaws and drive out illicit traders. He came with siege guns to reduce our Fort, which had been reported in Canada to be bristling with cannon and needle guns and he came and found open gates, a cripple as second in command, and 6 or 7 peaceable looking citizens. Our only armament were 2 old steamboat cannon and any amount of trade rifles, and our whiskey was cached on the bottom of Belly River.[89]

Traveling from the Flathead Valley to Fort Benton, Charles Schafft arranged his trip to temporary "exile" at Fort Whoop-Up in the summer of 1874 traveling up the Whoop-Up Trail. Along the way, Schafft became a most observant adventurer. The *River Press* brought his remarkable account to print as a "Literary Contribution by C.S.":

A Visit to "Whoop Up" in the Days Gone By.

The disturbed state of Indian affairs in Montana in 1874, made me desirous of viewing the investigations then in progress, from some other standpoint, and I finally came to the conclusion to disappear for a while across the border. Being greatly interested in the efforts, successes and failures attending the civilization of the aboriginal inhabitants, and somewhat tired of the society of mortals who, although no longer regarded as savages, were yet deemed but little above the brute, civilization having taking away what little romance attaches to the wild man. I determined to take a trip to Whoop Up, where I could see and meet the great North American in all his native glory and savage wildness. I had no apprehension in regard to the desperate whites who were supposed to be out there, and whom I might encounter, because having come to the mountains in early days, I was accustomed to the association of all sorts of characters and knew "roughing it" in all its phases. Accordingly, one fine day in the summer of "the year first above written," I found myself at the town of

Bull team from Fort Macleod loaded with wood and coal from Coalbanks, near Fort Whoop-Up. *Overholser Historical Research Center.*

Benton in search of an opportunity with which to convey myself to my destination. There was a sort of an irregular express run from Benton across the line in those days by the boys who were on the "trade," and having the advantage of being acquainted with some of the traders, I experienced no difficulty to secure a passage on the hurricane deck of a prairie schooner at an early day. My craft was commanded by Captain "Fred" [Henry Alfred Kanouse] who boasted of having one of the best prairie teams on the road, and I was told to be in readiness inside of twenty-four hours, and that we would whoop things up. Requesting one of my friends knowing in such matters, to fix up an outfit for me to take on the prairie, he judiciously selected and put up two or three gallons of whisky and an assortment of canned conveniences, advising me to be careful in regard to drinking the water to be met with. "It's regular pizen," said he, "to them that ain't use to it."

My captain and conveyance being ready to start, I was assigned a berth amidships with instructions to keep a good look out and hold on, because the fiery steeds would go like "blazes" after once being warmed up. I had some misgivings when the lash was applied and the word to go was given, on seeing the two lead horses turn around and look at the driver, while the wheelers were rubbing each other to save their hides from the whip; but after the expenditure of a voluminous volley of mixed expletives and some buck-skin, our cayuses finally seemed to know what was wanted, and headed for the Teton, at a pace that might have compared favorably with the slow and measured march of a funeral. "I know," said Fred, "what ails the horses, those confounded stable men kept them in the corral for the last four days, and they are hungry."

The first occasion I found to hold on and let go both at the same time, was going down to the Teton, when the wagon started down one coulee and the horses another. A small sage-brush saved an upset, but Fred was obliged to unload the wagon and pack the load to the bottom on his back. He had hoped to overtake some teams ahead of us going in the same direction, but as it was getting late, we encamped at the foot of the hill, Fred deploring the mishap, because he had hoped to be helped up the opposite side by the other teams. Next morning about daylight, we were awakened by an unearthly war-hoop, coming down the river, and immediately began to look for a hiding place among the sage, but the rattling of wheels soon after heard, informed us that a white party was approaching. And so, it was, some of the boys were going out on a trading expedition up the Teton, and having tendered us the morning cup agreed at once to help us up the next hill. Then, when nearing the Leavings, we saw the last one of the wagons ahead just starting up, and Fred urged his animals with all the art, in his power, but no use. A small mud-hole held on to the wheels, and the overhanging brush kept us from being seen, and we were left alone the second time to mourn the unloading of the wagon.

Having at last reached the middle of the hill, the cayuses concluded it was dinner time, and stopped to camp. Not being able to persuade them out of the notion, we unhitched and took a lunch ourselves, and how long we would have remained at this place, it is hard to tell, had not opportunely Captain Nelse [Narcisse Vielleaux] came along, who, assuming command for the time being, made the horses believe that he was a live Comanche, and they got away from him and up on the prairie with the load behind them very easily. Thanking the Captain for his courtesy, we traveled on over the smooth plain at a smart pace and overtook the outfits that night at Pend d'Oreille Springs. Fred was happy now, for other animals would assist him over slight elevations, and enable him to reach the end of his journey without much further jaw-breaking and expenditure of whip material. Our new comrades were evidently on the "trade" also. In jogging along they would frequently cast anxious looks behind, and in camp the distinguished name of Dusold [Indian Department detective Andrew Dusold] was often mentioned, but we met with no accidents or adventures worth mentioning the balance of the trip. Only at one place did I have to hold on with main strength; it was going down to the Marias, when a thunder storm coming from the south lashed up our team with lightning flashes, and caused them to exhibit a marvelous agility in the descent to the bottom.

The plain 200 miles north of Benton does not show many interesting features generally and we met with only a few small bands of bulls, some antelope, and further on the industrious badger, whose holes attracted the most attention.

When within a few miles of the St. Mary's at the junction of which with Belly river, Whoop-Up fort was situated, we met with the first indication of violence, by finding a dead Indian lying spread-eagle fashion in the center of the road. He could not have been exposed very long, for, exposed to the rays of the sun without any cover except a fragment of Uncle Sam's blue attached to an army button, decomposition had not yet taken place.

We reached [Fort] Whoop-Up. It was a large and solidly put-up trading post, the construction of which must have cost way up in the thousands. Situated as it was, in a broad flat, its inmates could easily stand off any number of hostiles contemplating an attack. A small graveyard on the outside attested the fact that not everyone who came to the country was permitted to return; but no inscription told the story of those who were here laid at rest.

My means of introduction having gained for me a temporary home at the fort, I soon became acquainted with some of the men who frequented it, and to my surprise found them to be what are generally called good and intelligent men, who could go to and return from the United States without hindrance at most times, and no reward was set upon the head of any of them. There was said to be only one man in that country who kept away from Uncle Sam's Territory on account of having committed a crime, and there were two or three deserters from the army who probably regretted having exchanged a life of comparative ease for one of disappointment and unforeseen hardship. Trade was conducted in the legitimate business principles of that day, and liquor was kept at the independent trading posts as an auxiliary, on the same conditions that the Hudson Bay Company kept it. At times a small camp trader would come in from across the line and exchange a mixture of pure alcohol and water with the Indians for robes, and the stimulant, acting upon the passions of savages, in heart hostile to each other, would result in a fight that sometimes would end in the death of one or both of the combatants.

At the time of my arrival an Indian had just met his fate from such a cause. Whoop-Up being a central region where the various tribes generally met, fights and battles between members of different bands took place occasionally without any other stimulus than natural animosity; and as those Indians do not bury their dead, bodies, skulls and skeletons could frequently be found. One day examining a rather poor specimen of cranium, I casually remarked that I would give four bits for a good one, and Billy, the oldest inhabitant out there, said he would get me one. Several days after he came in slightly "flushed," from another post, and emptying a gunny sack full of skulls at my feet, consolingly intimated that I would probably receive a wagon load in a few days, as he had told the boys that I had offered fifty cents apiece for them. That night the festive board was graced with a bottle adorned with an old scalp and skulls for candlesticks; but it was merely done as an illustration to show how Whoop-Up was painted by those who knew nothing of its realities.

An old preacher [undoubtedly Reverend John McDougall] traveling through the country, had met a lot of the boys just returning from a successful trading expedition, taking a slight recreation and feeling generally happy. He being evidently unused to the rough hospitality and expressions of frontier life, sent a lengthy report to the Canadian press painting a most fearful picture of outlawry and crimes committed upon the British Indians. Whoop-Up was pictured as an almost invincible stronghold, defended by hundreds of American renegades, and bristling with needle guns and cannon. This report, coming from religious sources, backed by interesting testimony of the Hudson Bay Company, gained credence, and the Canadian Government organized the Northwest Mounted Police for the purpose of driving out the American "freebooters."…

During my sojourn in that country there were but few white men from this side of the line in it, and only one fight occurred while I was there. It was at Kanouse's Fort, where, through some erroneous impressions a skirmish took place between the Kootenai's and the whites. The latter acted in self-defense, and after the termination of the misunderstanding, nearly blew up their whole establishment by the accidental discharge of a gun into a pan full of powder, while trying to demonstrate how the fight commenced. One or two Indians were killed on this occasion, and some of the whites, owing to the explosion slightly powder burned. Indeed, the whites did but little shooting at any time, unless it was to protect life and property.

Reports of the coming of the Police reached us now very frequently; those who had contraband in stock cached it; everything was quiet and trade nearly at a standstill, because no one knew to what extent the red-coats would interfere in business matters. At length a reliable messenger on running gear, came in and brought the intelligence that the force would be here in a few days. At last they arrived and encamped within a short distance of the Fort. On the following morning Col. Macleod, with about twenty mounted men, entered the Fort. He was met at the gate by Billy's little boy, whom he had decked with an old red uniform coat. There were only six or seven white men all told in the place, which had been painted as formidable.

The Col. entering the store implied that after a long prairie trip they were rather thirsty, and wanted to know if we couldn't come out with something to drink, but we had nothing and had tasted nothing of the kind since early that morning. He seemed to be a little disappointed and detailed three or four parties of his men to search the place, which being done, a Sergeant Major reported nothing contraband could be found. The Colonel, no doubt feeling very dry, and wishing besides doing his duty, probably to get hold of a good American drink to compare with Winnipeg poison, ordered another search to be made, which turned out as fruitless as the first one. While the rummaging was going on, I heard one policeman say to another, "Oh, if we only had the price set on some of these fellows' heads by the American Government, wouldn't we be fixed?" but then their impressions were new and based upon false reports. The Canadian authorities have long since learned that matters were not nearly so serious as painted. The police found that the men whom they had come to perhaps fight and conquer were peaceable traders, and the heavy siege guns brought along were useless; they had only affected the death of several horses dragging them over the prairie from Garry.

Since the establishment of Fort Macleod, Walsh and others, the relative positions of white persons have been slightly changed, but whether the Indian derived any benefits from the general changes accomplished, is doubtful, as they are reported to be in a starving condition today.

My time for disappearance having expired, I was glad now to take passage once more for Uncle Sam's dominions, and the name of "Whoop-Up" no longer excites my imagination with pictures of desperadoes and bloody deeds. C.S.[90]

Remarkable adventurer Charles Schafft summarized his return from "exile" in Whoop-Up Country, leaving Fort Whoop-Up on November 17, 1874:

I did not like the country much, and was glad to learn that Indian difficulties had ceased across the line. So, late in November 1 started back for the U.S. in Company of Johny Manning, "Big Sandy" Lane and Joe Bowers, and [Philander] Vogel. On Milk River we were caught in a terrible blizzard, and further advance with wagons had to be abandoned. Three of this party started back, and three of us concluded to come ahead, a conveyance was rigged up for me, and after a most perilous journey over the trackless prairie we arrived on the Marias, and reached the settlement on Sun River, from where I returned to Missoula by stage, to be employed as clerk again, by Agent Peter Whaley.[91]

Schafft's near-fatal return trip from Whoop-Up is dramatically described by him in two articles in Deer Lodge, Montana's newspaper *New North West*, titled a "Rough Trip."[92]

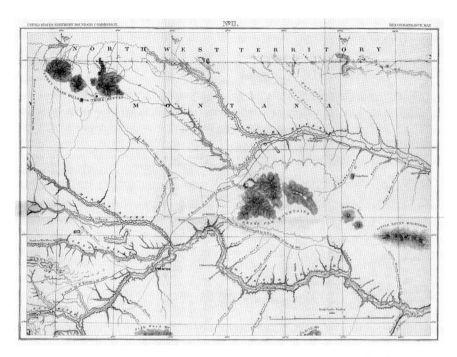

U.S. Northern Boundary Commission Survey Map No. 2 showing Whoop-Up Country from Fort Benton to Sun River Crossing and the eastern portion of the Whoop-Up Trail. *Author's collection.*

Whoop-Up stories continued to flow forth from the aging pioneers and writers hired by the Montana Newspaper Association, a news service that prepared four-page inserts for the weekly newspapers in Montana from 1920 to 1942. Each insert was loaded with historical articles, women's features, news updates and advertising. Martha Edgerton Rolfe Plassmann was among their most popular historical writers. A daughter of Montana's first territorial governor, Sidney Edgerton, Martha had a legendary knowledge of the pioneers and events from the territory's earliest days. In the following article, Martha Plassmann focused on one of the great freighters during the Whoop-Up era, James W. "Diamond R" Brown, who offered a new explanation for the "Whoop-Up" name.

The First Road to Traverse Blackfeet Reservation Led to Fort Whoop-Up

The Blackfeet reservation is today crossed and re-crossed by roads leading to Canada, and to the towns located on, or in the neighborhood of the reservation, and it is difficult to think of that section as it was sixty years ago. There are few men living who saw it then, and of these none is so qualified to tell of the second road across the reservation, as "Diamond R" Brown of Browning.…

James W. Brown was born Sept. 6, 1841, at Hillsboro, Ohio, fought in the Civil war, enlisting with the 20th Illinois Infantry, and serving until July, 1864. He was wounded at Fort Donelson, Shiloh, and Vicksburg, and was with Hancock's corps when Lincoln was killed. He was on duty at Washington until February, 1866, when he was mustered out at Camp Chase, Columbus, Ohio. He came West that year as a driver in a freight outfit, and has remained here ever since. Mr. Brown married a Blackfoot woman, and he and his family are now living on the reservation. He writes:

"When I came to Montana in 1866, the only road on the reservation was called the Red River Half Breed Cart Trail, which ran from Edmonton to Fort Benton [aka the Old North Trail]. It ran along at the foot of the mountains on the east side just outside the timber. It passed through Glacier National Park below the railroad station of the Great Northern. It then kept along the foot of the mountains clear to Fort Edmonton.

"In 1871 quite a trade sprung up here between the Fort Benton people and the northern Indians. Those of us who engaged in it at that time laid out another road leading from Fort Benton through to Canada. It came up the Teton about twenty-five miles, then left the Teton through the Knees and went on to the Marias.…

"Leaving the Marias it came up Medicine Rock Hill, as it was called. and from this hill crossed the bench to about where Shelby is now, and down onto Alkali Flat. It followed up the flat for fifteen miles in a northerly direction, when it left the flat and continued along what is called the Rocky Spring Ridge.

"From Rocky Spring Ridge it ran on north to what is known as Red River, or Dry Gulch. This name, the Indians told me, at the time, dated from a fight there between two big war parties, of Sioux and Crows who were attacked, or vice versa, by Piegans, Blackfeet, and Bloods. The battle was fiercely waged, and when it ended the creek ran red as if full of blood, and it has been called Red River ever since.

"After leaving Red River, the road kept on to what was called John Joe's Spring, and from there on to Milk River. Still going north, it crossed Eighteen Mile Coulee, continuing to Middle Coulee north to Kipp's Coulee. Leaving Kipp's Coulee it went on until it struck St. Mary's between St. Mary's and the forks of Belly River, which it forded at old Fort Whoop-Up, a branch running up to what is called Standoff at the present time. This is the first wagon road which ever crossed the reservation.

"When the Mounted Police came in 1874, there was another road laid out from Fort Shaw to McLeod, a mail route....

"[Signed] James W. Brown, better known as 'Diamond R. Brown.'"

I asked Mr. Brown the origin of the name "Whoop-Up." He answered that it was not to the interest of the large firms in Fort Benton to have others engage in the trade with the northern Indians, and they had men employed on the reservation to report those who attempted to cross it.

The "free lances" were forced to make their preparations secretly, such as buying the merchandise for the Indian trade, which in those days seems to have been chiefly alcohol or whiskey, and having loaded, they left Fort Benton at night, often traveling fifty miles or more without a stop, and "whooped it up for the Border." From this well-known fact came the name of the post.

Mr. Brown was in the Indian trade with Joseph Kipp on Belly River. Later he removed to Old Man River, where he was in business for himself. He seems to have done well there, until the coming of the Mounted Police, brought in by reports, had reached them, that liquor was being sold to the Indians. This was nothing new, as liquor had figured prominently in the fur trade on both sides of the line, and on both sides of the line it was illegal. It has been intimated that jealousy of the Hudson's Bay Company instigated the coming of the "Mounties."

In this instance they were expected and Mr. Brown had plenty of time to cache his store of the prohibited article before they arrived, under the leadership of Colonel MacLeod, who found everything all right at Mr. Brown's and the latter gentleman so hospitably disposed, that the Colonel spent the night with the man he had come to investigate.

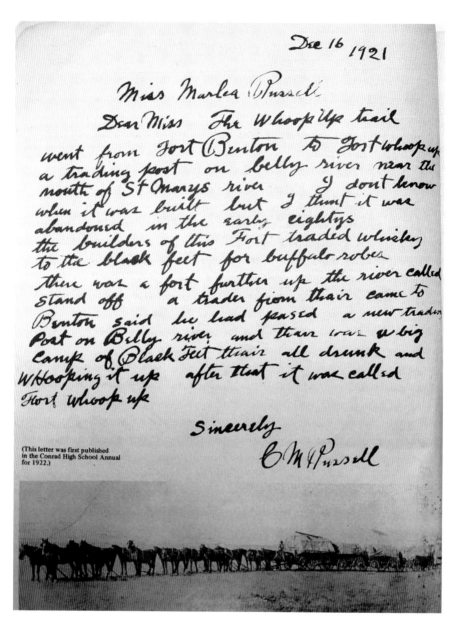

Dec 16 1921

Miss Marlea Russell

Dear Miss The Whoop Up trail went from Fort Benton to Fort Whoop up a trading post on belly river near the mouth of St Marys river I dont know when it was built but I think it was abandoned in the early eightys the builders of this Fort traded whiskey to the black feet for buffalo robes there was a fort further up the river called Stand off a trader from thair came to Benton said he had passed a new trading Post on Belly river and thair was a big camp of Black Feet thair all drunk and Whooping it up after that it was called Fort whoop up

Sincerely
C M Russell

(This letter was first published in the Conrad High School Annual for 1922.)

Charles M. Russell's letter about the Whoop-Up Trail sent in December 1921 to Marlea Russell, student at Conrad High School. *Conrad High School, The Whoop-Up Trail 1922.*

The next morning Colonel MacLeod, having mentioned that he wished to establish a post in the vicinity, Mr. Brown directed Charles Conrad who was also staying with him, to conduct the Colonel to the site of the present MacLeod, which was declared to be entirely satisfactory. From this it will be seen that the establishment of Fort MacLeod was due to the advice of two Montanans.

With the Mounted Police on the ground, there was no longer profit to be derived from the Indian trade, which Mr. Brown soon abandoned.

Few men have led such an adventurous life as James W. Brown, and none are more familiar with this northwestern country than he. Nearly eighty-five years of age, his mind is still active, and, although not physically strong, he enjoys, when in good mood, recounting his early experiences. He is a valuable link with the past—the past of the Civil war, in which he took such an active part, and the past of Montana's pioneer days.[93]

Conrad High School and the Whoop-Up Trail

The town of Conrad, named for trader William G. Conrad, near the site of historic Fort Conrad on the Whoop-Up Trail, shares with Fort Benton the lead in remembering and honoring the trail over the years. The Conrad Transportation and Historical Museum features the trail. In 1921, Conrad High School named its annual yearbook *The Whoop-Up Trail 1921*. Each year since then, the Conrad High School annual has borne that name.

The Whoop-Up Trail 1922 annual paid special tribute to the historic trail thanks to the initiative of an enterprising student, Marlea Russell, a junior in the class of '23. Marlea wrote a letter to famed cowboy artist Charles M. Russell asking about the history of the trail, and Charlie wrote this response, with yet another story about the naming of Whoop-Up:

Dec 16, 1921
Miss Marlea Russell

Dear Miss
The Whoop up trail went from Fort Benton to Fort Whoop up a trading post on the Belly river near the mouth of St Marys river.

I don't know when it was built but I think it was abandoned in the early eighties. The builder of this Fort traded whisky to the Black feet for Buffalo robes. There was a fort further up the river called Stand Off. A trader from thair came to Benton said he had passed a new trading post on the Belly river and their were a big camp of Black Feet all drunk and Whoopin it up. After that it was called Fort Whoop up.

Sincerely

C M Russell[94]

Using Charlie Russell's "history and other research," Marlea Russell wrote an article for the school annual:

The Whoop-Up Trail

The trail known as the "Whoop-Up Trail" passes through Pondera County about eighteen miles northeast of Conrad. This trail was used by the early freighters, with ox teams, who traded whiskey to the Blackfeet Indians in Canada for buffalo robes.

The Whoop-Up Trail runs from Fort Benton, the head of navigation on the Missouri river to a trading post on the Belly river, near the mouth of St. Mary's, in Alberta. It runs in a north-westerly direction from Fort Benton, crossing the Teton river at Narcisis Veyhues' [sic, Narcisse Vielleaux] ranch. He is better known as Captain Nels and tradition has it that he planted the bullberry bushes along the river

After crossing the Teton the trail keeps to its course, passing through Sollid and Fort Conrad. This fort is not standing now, but it was on the opposite side of the Marias river, from where Naismith is located. However, before coming to Fort Conrad, the trail crosses Pondera coulee at what is known as the "Leavings." This is where the Whoop-Up Trail meets a trail running to a trading post on Birch creek. Upon following the Whoop-Up trail further we find it crosses chimney Rock coulee and goes about two miles east of Shelby. It then runs to Ft. Whoop-Up in Canada.

The trail got its name through a very interesting incident. One day, a trader from Ft. standoff who came to Benton, told that he had passed a new trading post, on the Belly river, and that there

HUGE CROWD ENJOYS WHOOP-UP TRAIL DAYS FIRST ANNUAL FROLIC

The Lions club two day celebration of Whoop-Up Trail Days certainly went over with a bang and everyone in attendance was well satisfied with the first annual frolic in connection with this famous old time observance.

The setup for the celebration was in the city hall which was transformed into one large amusement place and with it went plenty of western atmosphere, dress and early day outfits, games and plenty of amusement.

tions from surrounding communities and towns and scores of Legionaires and their ladies present to help make it one enthusiastic frolic.

Saturday afternoon about four o'clock, the old-time parade was started through the downtown section and it was one of the best and most interesting that has ever swung down our city streets. The high school band was out despite the cold, high wind prevailing which failed to dampen their mus-

the general committee that had charge of the entire affair, wish to not only thank the various members who served on committees, but to all others who assisted in any manner.

Farm Security Makes Progress

Marked progress was made in

Fort Conrad Site Marker Dedicated

Project Part of Scouts' Tracing of Whoop-Up Trail

SHELBY — The recent dedication of an historical marker at the site of old Fort Conrad on the Marias River was a high point in a project started last spring by Boy Scouts of this area — the marking of the old Whoop-Up Trail.

The dedication, at the site of the old trading post 16 miles southeast of Shelby, was conducted by the Boy Scouts of the Nu Ooh Ska District (Toole, Pondera and Glacier Counties) and the Shelby History Group of the Montana Institute of the Arts.

The History Group provided all materials, as well as the plaque, for the marker. The Boy Scouts did all the work of erecting it.

The scouters also did all the work of locating the site of the fort, one of the main waypoints on the Whoop-Up Trail, the old wagon freight road between Fort Benton in Montana and Fort Whoop-Up, near Lethbridge in Alberta, Canada.

Built in 1875

Fort Conrad was built in 1875 by Sol Abbott and Henry Powell for I. G. Baker & Co. of Fort Benton as a trading post and stopping place for the wagon trains to Fort Whoop-Up. The fort was in existence for 15 years. When the Great Falls & Canada narrow gauge railway came through the area in 1890, wagon freighting came to an end. Over the years the buildings disappeared.

The fort was named for Charles Conrad, its first manager. There was no blockhouse at Fort Conrad, as that time it was customary to designate trading posts as forts. Fort Conrad had a store, warehouse, dining room, lodging house, dwellings, corrals and barns. Indians and trappers, as well as the wagon freighters, traded at the fort.

In 1879 Fort Conrad was sold to Joe Kipp. He made many improvements and even built a sawmill. James Willard Schultz, well-known author, lived there about that time. In the early 1880's, soldiers from Fort Shaw did the rounding Indian stragglers from the reservations patrolled the area and camped at the F Ranch three miles downriver from the fort.

Joe Kipp sold the fort to Jim McDevitt in 1895. Mike Connelly leased the fort in 1898 and lived there until 1899.

During the search for the fort site, Mike Connelly's son and daughter were of great assistance to the scouts. Connelly's son, Tom, now lives in Shelby and his daughter is Mrs. Johnnie Sullivan of Great Falls.

Trails Award

Scout leaders Pat Sanderson of Oilmont and Pat Kelley of Sunburst were the originators of the idea of marking the Whoop-Up Trail, which led to their being interested in having their troop, No. 72 of Sunburst,

UNVEILING—Boy Scout leaders and members of the Shelby History Group of the Montana Institute of the Arts are pictured as they unveiled a permanent marker erected by the Scouts and the History Group at the site of old Fort Conrad, Marias River trading post on the Whoop-Up Trail from 1875 to 1890. From left are Lee Eilert, Milk River, Alberta, scoutmaster; Mrs. Ralph Benjamin, past president, and Mrs. Clifford D. Coover, president, of the History Group; Tom Connelly, who as a boy lived at Fort Conrad; Wilbur Werner, Cut Bank, chairman of the Nu Ooh Ska Boy Scout district; Helen West, Cut Bank historian who gave the main address at the dedication, and Pat Sanderson, Oilmont, district organization chairman and co-originator of the Scouts' project to mark the Whoop-Up Trail. Wallace Ruetten photo.

PLAQUE—At right is the plaque on the Fort Conrad marker. Gus Coolidge, Sunburst, lettered the scroll which is under a fiberglass case made by the Rev. Julius Hovland, Lutheran pastor at Sunburst. Paul Dube, Shelby, did the Whoop-Up trail drawing at the base. Wallace Ruetten photo.

Cover Photo

A Boy Scout color guard lowers the flag to mark the completion of the ceremony dedicating the marker at the site of Fort Conrad, on the Marias River 16 miles southeast of Shelby. Wallace Ruetten photo.

SITE OF FORT CONRAD 1875-1890

An Important Blackfeet Indian Fur-Trading Post and Stop-over Point for Wagon-Trains Traveling the Whoop-Up Trail from Ft. Benton, Montana to forts Whoop-Up and McLeod, Alberta.

Marker Placed August 4, 1963, by Boy Scouts of America, of Nu-ooh-ska District, and Shelby History Group. M.I.A.

work toward the Historic Trails Award of the national Boy Scouts.

"Where to start on something like this was anybody's guess," Sanderson says. "We knew little about the trail but knew it was

Continued on page 11

18—GREAT FALLS TRIBUNE, SUNDAY, OCTOBER 19, 1963

Above: Reporting the first annual Whoop-Up Trail Days in Conrad in 1939. *From the* Conrad Independent, *April 20, 1939.*

Left: Boy Scouts dedicating marker at the site of Fort Conrad on Old Whoop-Up Trail. *From the* Great Falls Tribune, Montana Parade, *October 20, 1963.*

was a large camp of Blackfeet there. All drunk and whooping it up. After that the fort was known as Fort Whoop-Up. The trail was also given this name.

It is not known when this trail was built, but it is believed to have been abandoned in the early eighties, when Montana was still a territory.

MARLEA RUSSELL, '23.

Authorities: C.M. Russell, Great Falls, Montana; A.J. Fowler, Devon, Montana.[95]

CONRAD'S WHOOP-UP TRAIL DAYS

The town of Conrad continued to lead in promoting remembrance of the Whoop-Up era in 1939 when it presented the first annual two-day celebration of "Whoop-Up Trail Days." In April, Conrad City Hall became one large amusement venue organized by the Lions Club and featuring a Friday night western costume dance followed by a Saturday afternoon parade with an

Reconstructed Fort Whoop-Up, 2005. *Photo by author.*

old-time western theme. Building on the success of this first Trail Days, the event has continued each year since. The Whoop-Up Trail is alive and well in Conrad, Montana.[96]

Remembered in Lethbridge

Both Lethbridge and Fort Benton newspapers publish articles and the towns hold events relating to Whoop-Up Country and the Trail on occasion, as in this account of the Fort Benton–Fort Macleod Trail as part of an Old Trails series in the *Lethbridge Herald* in 1948. This article mentions Nicholas Sheran's sister, Marcella Sheran, as the first white woman to travel over the Whoop-Up Trail. Filled with inaccuracies, it stresses the violence, the whisky and the "most utterly depraved and lawless" characters to the extreme.

The Old Trails—No. 7 Ft. Benton–Ft. Macleod [originally, Whoop-Up Trail]
By E. Lynch—Staunton

This old historic trail, the oldest of them all, was to begin with merely a war-trail used by savage and painted Indians on the warpath. But for long years it was the only beaten track leading into the Blackfoot country of the Canadian North West Territories, and was as dangerous to venture over as being in direct line of the darting fangs of an infuriated rattlesnake.

The Blackfeet were fiercely savage. They resented any intrusion into their territory whatsoever, and were notoriously keen of sight. Anyone who ventured to enter there was taking his life in his hands. But as always men will risk life, everything, for gold.

A party of prospectors in search of gold was reputedly the first to venture within this territory, to be followed by the ubiquitous trader, who, to placate the savagery of the Indian, brought "firewater" and proceeded to despoil him.

The trader found a treasure trove of furs rather than of gold, and soon he was bringing caravans of goods, contraband though they might be and undoubtedly were, to trade for the wealth of furs.

And so, the famous trail over which during the last quarter of the nineteenth century, men famous and infamous were to pass, was begun. What tragedies, what savagery have been enacted along its course, what feats of endurance and acts of heroism we shall perhaps never know more than a moiety of! Thenceforth, the trail became more and more deeply indented as the bull teams, hauling the creaking wagons in long strings, wound their tedious way up hill and downhill, seeking always the easiest route.

They came from Ft. Benton, a trading post 85 miles south of the international boundary, then a very doubtful and mostly unrecognized line. Ft. Benton was the head of navigation on the Missouri river, a town of notorious saloons lining the river front. It was the home of many dashing frontiersmen and traders, also of many dangerous characters and gun-toters. But these were the men who had the hardihood and temerity to venture within the Blackfoot territory for the purpose of trade which in spite of the attending risks proved tremendously profitable.

In 1865 [*sic*, 1870] the first six-bull team hauling a wagonload of trade goods was brought in by two traders, Alf Hamilton and John Healy. They traveled from Ft. Benton [*sic*, Sun River Crossing] northward for something like 200 miles until they came to the junction of the Belly and St. Mary's rivers where they established a trading post which they named Ft. Hamilton.

The Indians came readily enough to trade and to carouse— the Blackfeet, the Bloods, the Peigans, the Stonies, and also their natural and hereditary enemies, the Crees. Battles were fought before and about the post, they stole each other's horses and lay in ambush for surprise attacks, and finally a massacre was staged. The Cree party was annihilated, the Blackfeet taking many scalps, capturing horses and making the Cree women their prisoners.

The frightful orgies constantly in progress ended with the looting and burning of the post in 1869 [*sic*, 1870]. The white men barely escaped with their lives, and made their way as best they could back over the long and dangerous trail to Ft. Benton. But in 1871 [*sic*, 1870] the post was rebuilt and named Ft. Whoop-Up from the vicious ribaldry that was enacted there.

The new fort was built by William Gladstone, a hardy adventuring spirit of those early days. It was strongly constructed within a high stockade with bastions and ramparts loopholed and brass cannon mounted at two opposite corners. The Indians were fearful of the man-made thunder of the guns and thereafter the fort managed to hold its own against them. Though tragedy was ever at hand, as when two traders, Dave Akers, a notorious tough picturesque character, who was known as a gun-toter and a killer, and [Tom] Purcell, his partner, also of notorious fame, quarreled. They fought a duel [much later in 1894] in which Akers was killed.

...Over 400 men, nearly all of the most utterly depraved and lawless character, were known to have been engaged in the trade of such contraband goods as liquor, tobacco, guns and ammunition.

The tremendous stocks of furs that were taken out of the country during these years, buffalo robes and wolf skins mostly were freighted to Ft. Benton. Early in the spring the trains again started north, the wagons heavily loaded with goods for trade. [*sic*, Actually, the trains moved southeast to Fort Benton in the spring loaded with the winter's robes, while wagons moved northwest in the fall taking goods for the winter trade.] Such goods being kegs of rum [*sic*, whisky] which were diluted with water in the proportion of one to one hundred in trade, sugar, syrup and flour in barrels, blankets of gaudy hue, cloth, print, brass rings and glass beads.

For greater safety the caravans or trains were as large as possible sometimes consisting of as many as eight teams, a team being composed of 12 to 15 yoke of oxen, or mules, hauling three wagons strung out one after another and carrying in all 21,000 pounds of freight. The drivers of the teams, one to each team, were known as "bullwhackers." Usually they walked beside their teams carrying heavily loaded bullwhips which they cracked like pistol shots over the backs of the animals. It is claimed an expert bullwhacker would pick a fly off the furthest animal with the loaded thong of his whip, or in lieu of the fly a piece of hide. They plodded along at the painfully slow rate of 12 to 15 miles a day the entire trip of some 200 miles taking about 14 days. With mules which were used later the trip was made in from eight to ten days, and by horses with the stage carrying mail, or by horseback, in from four to six days.

At night camp was made beside the trail, the wagons drawn up into a circle forming a sort of barricade. There were a number of saddle horses in the outfit and riders to herd the animals constantly as they grazed during the night and to guard against Indian attack.

One man was held off to cook for the train; he did nothing else; and buffalo chips were used for fuel where there was no wood. Game—buffalo and antelope—was always plentiful along the route. In fact, caravans have been known to be brought to a standstill for hours and days by the passing of tremendous herds of buffalo.

The wagons were strong and were built entirely of wood with never a nail in them. Even the wheels were not iron-rimmed but were bound with tough raw hide. Their creaking was unceasing.

Day in and day out it was creak! Creak! Creak! As the oxen laboriously plodded along the trail, the bullwhackers snapping their long whips and giving voice to a characteristic language understandable only by the cattle they were prodding on, though seemingly having but little effect on them.

Slow but sure they were, even if they did cross a stretch of quaking bog and quagmire, where the wheels sank to the hubs in black oozy mud or sucking clay, the oxen, though they went almost out of sight themselves, pulled them through; or scrambling over the rolling boulders of a swift stream where the animals had to swim, yet they eventually dug their cloven hoofs in the loose gravel of the opposite side and hauled the wagons, dripping cascades of water out of the bottoms whether the banks were precipitous or not.

With the passing of every train, the ruts became deeper. There was no mistaking the trail, except when it was covered with deep snow or a blizzard was raging.

Dr. [John W.] Dawson the eminent English geologist, writes of travelling over this trail in the early eighties. He and his party camped on the west side of the Sweet Grass Hills, three notable elevations or isolated mountain peaks rising out of the prairie. Ten miles further on they came upon the bodies of a number of Indians of the Crow tribe, left unburied but scalped, obviously the victims of Indian warfare.

From the Sweet Grass Hills, always a welcome landmark in a land of few prominent headlands, the trail crossed the Milk

River, and mounted the low-lying Milk River Ridge, its numerous springs serving as excellent camping places though there were several deep coulees cutting into the ridge to be avoided. Then they headed for the Peace Buttes of Indian fame, in a northwesterly direction. Further to the northward, the Porcupine Hills rose into view. Always a watch was kept at the Fort, and as the team mounted the crest of the hills ten miles away and came into sight it was the custom to fire a salute of guns in welcome.

Nicholas Sheran came to Ft. Whoop-Up with the Healys and Hamilton about 1867 [*sic*, 1870] over the Ft. Benton trail, and near the location of the Fort discovered the first coal found in Alberta. Until 1882 he was engaged in the mining business at Coalbanks (now Lethbridge) and shipped thousands of tons of coal by bull team over the Ft. Benton trail to Ft. Benton where it was re-shipped down the river even as far as St. Louis. Sheran was drowned in 1882 while assisting a party of North West Mounted Police under Col. Macleod, to cross the Old Man river below Ft. Whoop-Up during high water and his body was never recovered.

Two years after his arrival [in 1872], his sister, Marcella Sheran came to keep house for her brother. Miss Sheran was undoubtedly the first white woman to travel over the Ft. Benton trail. We wonder what she must have thought of it—the slow plodding oxen, the rough jolting of the "dead-axe" wagons their everlasting creaking, the constant hazard of Indian attack with the added contingency of losing one's scalp.

Always at the mercy of the elements—rain, and snow, sun and wind…and how the wind can blow over those open plains— the discomfort of camping on the trail often with but a scant supply of water and fuel. There was the notably superb scenery of sufficient compensation—the Rockies rimming the western sky in their picturesque, the prairie melting into the blue of the horizon to the eastward, the deeply-rutted trail winding over hill and dale in an ever-changing vista, the glory of a sunrise on the trail, a sunset as the day's halt was made. The thrill of sighting the unique Sweet Grass Hills—the "Montagnes de Foin de Senteur" as the hunters of the plains named them because they were clothed with an abundance of sun-cured grass; crossing the boggy river bottoms, the treacherous currents of the streams;

then winding, winding over Milk River Ridge—scars of the old trail may be found there to this day, though unfortunately the old Ft. Benton Trail unlike the roads built by the Romans, is entirely impracticable as a modern highway.

Ten or 12 halts would be necessary along the way and camp made each time. Would they become deadly monotonous in their repetition or was each a new experience in itself?

As the Milk River Ridge is mounted, before lay the Peace Buttes. It is Indian territory, dangerous ground, of misleading legend ranging from Bull's Head Butte to the Sand Hills, a long way further eastward where the Indian rides on his last, long gallop—"death." The tension grows tighter. The scalped and mutilated body lying close by the trail may be redman or paleface, but always it is scalped!

The cracking of the bullwhackers' whips is like a fusillade of pistol shots, their language has the scorching blast of a prairie fire as they desperately urge their teams to an infinitesimally faster pace. Painfully slow the teams mount to the crest, but surely. Ten miles away they are sighted at the fort. They hear the welcoming salute of the guns. They are almost safe.

And so the furrows of the trail grew deeper and deeper with the great wave of prosperity that was sweeping up the Missouri River to Ft. Benton and on to Ft. Whoop-Up.

But this prosperity was almost the undoing of the redman. The Indians were fast becoming utterly demoralized. In truth the traders were more to blame for the savageness of these people than were the savages themselves, for the Indians soon realized that they were being exploited and cheated and robbed of their furs, their horses, their women, even their manhood. They hated and resented these white traders, but they craved the raw liquor they brought them.

Ft. Whoop-Up was headquarters for trade in the south, just as Ft. Edmonton was for the Hudson Bay Company in the north. The Indians brought their furs and horses to trade, and camped in great numbers about the gates of the Fort, though they were not allowed to enter, the trading being conducted entirely through a small wicket. But outside the gates frightful orgies of war dances and tribal rituals were constantly in progress, as the Indians crazed by the liquor doled out to them in trade gambled their last possession. Many of the traders acquired by purchase Indian wives who acted as a sort of buffer against the savagery and lawlessness of the Indians.

The Indians vie with one another in having the greatest number of scalps dangling from their belts and white men's scalps ranked high. When Trader Howell Harris was approaching the Fort in 1871, a Frenchman of his train was shot at the very gates.

Ft. Kipp and Ft. Conrad were built by the I.G. Baker Company of Ft. Benton but both forts were destroyed shortly afterwards. The T.C. Power Company also traded at these forts from Fort Benton. Forts Stand Off, Slide-Out and Whisky Gap, built about the year 1872, are all reminiscent of those liquor-trading days along the Ft. Benton Trail.

In 1874 the first company of the North West Mounted Police in their march westward across the plains came upon the Ft. Benton trail by which route they travelled northward to Ft. Whoop-Up. Col. Macleod made an offer to Akers, who was then in charge, to buy the fort, but his offer of $10,000 being refused, the company continued on up the Old Man river to the site where Fort Macleod was established as the first police post in the North West Territories. The second contingent of the N.W.M.P. in 1874 [*sic*, 1875] entrained from Chicago to St. Louis, then came up the Missouri River by boat to Ft. Benton, from which disembarking point they came by the old Ft. Benton Trail to Ft. Macleod. [Two contingents of Mounted Police recruits came upriver to Fort Benton in 1875: thirty-five Mounted Police arrived on June 22 on the Fontenelle; thirty Mounted Police commanded by Colonel Irvine arrived on June 26 on the Josephine along with Norman T. Macleod, nephew of Colonel James F. Macleod.]

Now that they were established, it was the determined intention of the police to stop the illicit trading of liquor with the Indians. But the traders had their scouts, too, and on the approach of the police soon acquired the habit of hiding their stocks of liquor and contraband goods in caches under the banks of the river. On a later visit to Ft. Whoop-Up by Col. Macleod with an escort of Mounted Police and Jerry Potts as guide and interpreter, they found the Fort deserted and the bodies of four Indians lying unburied within the stockade.

In the fall of 1874, Capt. Denny of the N.W.M.P., with two constables and Jerry Potts as guide was sent to Ft. Benton to arrange for a supply of forage for their horses to be freighted over the old trail to Ft. Macleod. It was a dismal journey. The country had been burned over by prairie fire and there was no grazing for their horses. The weather turned very cold and had it not been for finding a cache of provisions left in hiding along the way as was the custom of the country in those days, they would have perished. The snow became so deep it was impossible to see the trail, but Jerry Potts guided them safely to the foot of the Sweet Grass Hills where they camped overnight under their shelter, then on to Ft. Benton.

On their way back, they stopped at Ft. Whoop-Up where D.W. Davis, who was later to become the first federal member for the territory of Alberta, was in charge with fresh vegetables and native fruits. Mr. Davis was soon after sent to Ft. Macleod as manager of the I.G. Baker store there.

But with the coming of the police and the prohibition of liquor in trade with the Indians, Ft. Whoop-Up was doomed. Besides the buffalo had now disappeared and the Indians no longer had robes to trade, though there was still much trading and thieving in horses.

The whisky traders tried to outwit the police, for which purpose the Forts Stand Off, Slide-Out and Whisky Gap had been built, but against the strength and righteousness of the police their efforts were not very effective. The days of the whisky trader and the infamous Fort Whoop-Up were indeed over.

Many a pioneer has entered Alberta by this famous and picturesque old route. The Marquis of Lorne, governor-general of Canada, when he visited the North West Territories in 1881, attended by an escort of Mounted Police, was filled with delight as he journeyed over the old Ft. Benton Trail by way of Ft. Benton and down the Missouri River by boat. F.W. Godsal, one of the first ranchers in southern Alberta, accompanied by Capt. and Mrs. Scobie, entered the Territory of Alberta in 1882 on the 24th of May (then known as the Queen's Birthday and an important occasion in British dominions) by way of the Ft. Benton Trail.

John Herron of Pincher Creek, an original member of the N.W.M.P. of 1874, and later Member of Parliament, on an occasion in 1875, rode alone from the international boundary to Ft. Macleod over the Ft. Benton Trail and through hostile Indian country.

And so, the old trail has in its day been both famous and infamous, and there have passed over it many illustrious and distinguished persons, though it is now but a memory.

But it is yet well worth travelling over in the present day by way of the Sunshine Trail, the highly modernized highway that most closely follows the course of the old Ft. Benton Trail, coming from the international border from Coutts with the unique Sweet Grass Hills in full view to the eastward and the superb Big Chief Mountain dominating the scene to the westward with the wondrously beautiful Waterton Lakes lying before it; along the course of the Milk River with its mysterious Picture Rocks and Bad Lands; beyond the Milk River Ridge and the historic Indian Peace Buttes, and by the low-lying Lake Pakowki, lower than the bed of the Milk River, to be seen in the distance; on through the wide fertile lands, the wheat fields and the sugar beet lands,

Fort Benton to Fort Macleod Trail Marker on the steamboat levee in Fort Benton. *Overholser Historical Research Center.*

Bob Doerk, eloquent living history presenter and friend of the Blackfoot, at Old Fort Benton posed with the Chief Joseph Surrender Rifle, in the collection of the River & Plains Society. *Photo by Craig and Liz Larcom.*

soon all to be brought under irrigation; and on to Lethbridge, near where the notorious trading post of Ft. Whoop-Up once flourished on its precincts, and the Indians hunted the buffalo in their thousands and fought their tribal wars.

You will be traveling through the land of the Chinook and once again along the ancient course of the old Fort Benton trail—by the Sweet Grass Hills, over the Milk River Ridge, past the site of the old trading post where, in fact, traders and redmen did once "whoop it up." Then on to Ft. Macleod, the earliest post of the present day Royal Canadian Mounted Police force.[97]

Six years later, in 1954, it was Fort Benton's turn to remember and pay tribute to the Fort Benton–Whoop-Up/Fort Macleod Trail. On this occasion, Fort Benton invited Canadians from both Alberta and Saskatchewan to join in ceremonies for a new trail marker, dedicated by Montana governor J. Hugo Aronson. The *River Press* reported on the festivities, including a remarkable speech by Mayor G. Rider Davis of Fort Macleod, the son of Whoop-Up trader Donald W. Davis.

DEDICATION OF WHOOP-UP TRAIL MARKER

On July 4, 1954, Canadians joined with residents of Fort Benton to dedicate a prominent marker to commemorate the Fort Benton–Fort Macleod Trail marker and the long-shared past of Fort Benton with the provinces of Alberta and Saskatchewan. The principal speech on this occasion was delivered by Mayor G. Rider Davis of Fort Macleod, a son of D.W. Davis, who traded at Fort Whoop-Up and in Whoop-Up Country. Two members of the Royal Canadian Mounted Police from Lethbridge—Corporal A.E. Dickinson and Constable C.R. Kvern—also attended the three-day celebration.

The dedication program was attended by Montana governor Hugo Aronson, and the marker was presented to the state by Professor Verne Dusenberry of Montana State College in Bozeman, a former president of the Montana Institute of Arts.

Engraved on a plaque imbedded in the marker is this story:

> The Fort Benton to Fort Macleod or "Whoop-Up" Trail into Canada was the main artery of commerce in the 1869–1883 era. Twenty yoke of oxen was a team and each team hauled three of the heavy freight wagons loaded with trade goods, calico and whiskey. They returned loaded with hides for the St. Louis market. Until the closing of the river trade this road was the source of supply for the Royal Canadian Mounted Police, the boundary survey and the Canadian Pacific Railway. The resourceful, fearless plainsmen and bullwhackers relaxed at the end of their hazardous journey, opened up their cargo—not the calico—and "whooped it up." Thus, the name "Fort Whoop-Up" and the famous "Whoop-Up Trail."

A pageant, *Tall Tales of Fort Benton*, directed by Professor Bert Hansen of Montana State College, was presented in Fort Benton's outdoor arena on Friday, Saturday and Sunday. It colorfully portrayed scenes from the old Fort Benton territory.[98]

"WHOOP-UP TRAIL" SPEECH BY DAVIS
Canadian's Account of History of Famed North to Canada Road

The *River Press* is printing below the speech made by Mayor G. Rider Davis of Fort Macleod on the occasion of dedication of the "Whoop-Up Trail" marker at Fort Benton July 4th. Mayor Davis is not only an authority on the history of the trail north out of Fort Beaton to Canada, but is a son of one of the men who pioneered the route.

Text of the speech was unavailable at the time of the dedication, but publication now will, we believe, be of interest to many readers.

I consider it a privilege to be here today and I wish to thank the Fort Benton History Intertest Group of the Montana Institute of Arts and the City of Fort Benton for the honour they have conferred on me by asking me to speak on the occasion of the dedication of the marker to indicate the beginning of the Whoop-Up Trail. I also wish to congratulate the citizens of Fort Benton on their enterprise in placing such a marker to commemorate this Trail which is unique for many reasons. I had the pleasure of attending the 100th anniversary celebration here in 1946 and I know that this celebration aroused an interest in the past which is very gratifying, as it stimulated the desire to preserve the records of early days, which otherwise might soon be lost forever.

"The Whoop-Up Trail" almost automatically calls to mind "Whisky Traders," and we are only too prone to associate that trade alone with the trail and to think of it in terms of contraband and violence. Actually, the whisky trade was only incidental in the history of this trail. Its origin is found long before the time the white men came, in the trail that was beaten down by roving bands of Indians travelling backwards and to rewards, north and south. This was the path that was followed by the traders, and it became the first international highway in this part of the country between two great and friendly nations. It was of the utmost importance to both State and Province in their development from small pioneer settlements. It became a great avenue of trade and commerce providing an outlet for the commodities that were freighted up the Missouri River by river boats and in return furs and buffalo robes were carried south and the coal from Canada provided grateful warmth for many a resident of old Fort Benton. For a large part of the heyday of the Whoop-Up Trail, approximately fifteen years from 1867 to 1884, it was a veritable lifeline for the small Canadian communities that grew up following the arrival of the N.W.M.P. in 1874. From Winnipeg, the nearest Canadian base of supplies, the trip across the prairies was long and wearisome, so in a day when there were no Banks and no Post Offices in Alberta. not only was the Whoop-Up Trail the route by which food and clothing, the necessities of life as well as the luxuries, were brought in, but it was also the chief means of communication with Eastern Canada.

Much of the colour and romance of our immediate past is associated with this trail over which there travelled the swiftly moving vehicles of the whisky traders, the heavily laden bull trains and the picturesque stage coaches. Indeed, this trail is haunted by a colourful array—Indians and traders, red coated mounties, missionaries and rivermen, settlers of every sort who all had a part in the building of the Canadian and American West.

With this dedication today, the Trail is well marked from beginning to end. A few years ago the Jaycees of Lethbridge set up a marker to indicate the site of the old Fort Whoop-Up, near Lethbridge; there is a humorous reference to the trail near Conrad, which I am sure many of you have read, and in September, 1952, the Historic Sites and Monuments Board of Canada unveiled a monument at Coutts, Alberta, at the approximate place where the trail crossed the border, so that we have a rough idea of the general course followed by the trail. To give you a picture of this route, I know no better way than to quote a paragraph from an article written by Paul F. Sharp, Associate Professor of History at Iowa State College, who did a great deal of careful research in connection with the Whoop-Up Trail.

"Two hundred and forty miles northwest of Benton lay Fort Macleod; northern terminus of the Whoop-Up Trail. Snakelike, the trail crawled out along the banks of the Teton River to the Whoop-Up Crossing on Captain Nelse's ranch, then it struck out across the plains passing Pen d'Oreille Springs on Yeast Powder Flat to cross the Marias River near old Fort Conrad. Northward the trail swept past Rocky Springs in northern Montana to enter Canada near present day Sweet Grass (and Coutts). In Canadian territory the trail forded the Milk River, crossed the St. Mary's River by Fort Whoop-Up, then continued across the Belly River to Fort Macleod on the Oldman River."

This description agrees point for point with an account written over 70 years ago, in the diary of Frank White, who came in to Fort Macleod and Calgary over the Whoop-Up Trail.

"Sept. 7th, 1882 left Fort Benton at 4:30 P. M. and camped on north shore of Teton River.

"Sept. 8th, drove from the Teton to Nelse's or the Leavings of the Teton where the trail left the river and struck out across the prairie.

"Sept. 9th, drove from Pend d'Oreille to Kipp's at the Marias River.

"Sept. 10th, left Kipp's at the Marias River to Rocky Springs.

"Sept. 11th, left Rocky Springs and travelled to the north side of Milk River.

"Sept. 12th, left Milk River and travelled to the south side of St. Mary's River and Sept. 13th, drove from St. Mary's River to Fort Macleod on the Oldman River."

The trip from Fort Benton to Fort Macleod which then took about six days can now be made in a matter of hours.

In September 1874, 80 years ago, after their arduous march of almost 3 months across the Canadian prairies, the North West Mounted Police were at a loss where to turn to reach their objective, the notorious Fort Whoop-Up. Col. French and Col. Macleod decided to go south to Fort Benton "to communicate with Ottawa and to procure provisions and information. On 29th September word came from Col. Macleod at Benton that we were only forty miles from Fort Whoop-Up. We were instructed to move camp about 15 miles west, a well-beaten trail leading to that notorious rendezvous from Benton. This trail had been continuously used for several years by traders going back and forth and was here clearly defined. The news was most welcome.

While in Benton the Commissioner had contracted with I.G. Baker & Company to furnish all requirements of the force in the south for a year and a loaded bull team was now on the way out. In these words in "The Law Marches West," Sir Cecil Denny gives a first hand account of traffic with the Police over the Whoop-Up Trail. Even while they were on their way to their new home at Fort Macleod, an enterprising trader from Fort Benton passed them with a load of goods to set up trade wherever the force made its headquarters.

Of the beginning of the trail—Fort Benton, there is nothing that I could tell that you do not already know, but I would like to speak for a few minutes of the Canadian end of the trail—Fort Whoop-Up, most notorious of all the whisky forts in Southern Alberta. The location of this fort is about 7 miles South West of the City of Lethbridge at the junction of the St. Mary's and Belly Rivers. The original edifice called Fort Hamilton, was built some time between 1867 and 1869 by John J. Healy and A.B. Hamilton and was destroyed by fire in 1871. In the same year a new fort was built about 300 feet north of the original one. This was built under the supervision of William Gladstone a former Hudson's Bay Company boat builder and it was very strongly constructed. The most publicized description of this Fort is one given by Major General Sir Samuel B. Steele in his book "Forty Years in Canada." He was an original member of the 1874 N.W.M.P. and was a Sergeant Major at that time in the historic march of 1000 miles across the western plains:

"One of the principal posts of the traders in that region was Fort Hamilton, commonly known as 'Whoop-Up' situated at the forks of the Belly and St. Mary's Rivers. There were two walls, about a dozen feet apart, built of heavy squared logs, braced across by heavy log partitions about the same distance from one another, dividing it into rooms, which were used as dwellings, blacksmiths' shop, stores, etc. the doors and windows opening into the square. There were bastions at the corners and the walls were loop-holed for musketry. Iron bars were placed across the chimneys to prevent the Indians from getting in that way. There were heavy logs across the partitions and a strong gate of oak, with a small opening to trade through. All other posts merely had palisades, but they were strong enough for the purpose. The trader stood by at the wicket, a tubful of whisky stood by him, and when an Indian pushed in a buffalo robe to him through the hole in the wall he handed out a tin cupful of the poisonous decoction. A quart of the stuff bought a fine pony. When spring came, wagonloads of the proceeds of the traffic were escorted to Fort Benton, Montana, some 200 odd miles south."

There are various versions of how the fort got its name, one of the best known being that John Power, brother of T.C. Power, on one occasion asked how things were going up north and was told "Oh, they're whooping it up," so Fort Whoop-Up it became. There is a poem by Stephen St. Vincent Benet, which, with some variation is quite appropriate in this connection:

"I have fallen in love with American names,
Sharp names that never grow fat,
The snakeskin titles of mining claims,
The plumed war bonnet of Medicine Hat,
Whoop-Up and Standoff and Whisky Gap."

I have visited this historic site, twice in recent years, once with a nephew of Col. James F. Macleod, Norman Macleod, who had worked for the I.G. Baker Company in old Fort Macleod and who had driven on different occasions from Fort Macleod to Fort Benton over the Whoop-Up Trail. We came in from Lethbridge on that occasion by car, but recent floods have cut away the river banks and made that route impassable. Last October, in company with Ex-Commissioner Stuart T. Wood and Corporal Shaw of the R.C.M.P. and a pioneer son of Alberta, Norman Grier, we came in over the Blood Indian Reservation to the top of the high bank overlooking the Whoop-Up river bottom and from there we could see the outline of the old fort. The site is marked by the marker put up by the Jaycees of Lethbridge and the old well is still there. The only approach to the old fort now is by going down the steep hill on foot.

No tale of the Whoop-Up Trail would be complete without a reference to the men who made the trail as we know it. Many of these men became prominent citizens of Montana and Southern Alberta and their names are identified with our pioneer history. Healy and Hamilton, Akers and Gladstone, come to mind when we think of Whoop-Up. John J. Healy, trader, sheriff, newspaper publisher and prospector, was typical of many a pioneer to whom new horizons continually beckoned. As a boy, I remember him in Dawson City, Y.T., where he was the general manager of the North American Transportation and Trading Company at the time of the Yukon Gold Rush. His partner, A.B. Hamilton, afterwards served in the Montana legislature for two terms. Nicholas Sheran whose coal banks supplied the return load for the bull teams, was drowned in 1882, while assisting a party of Police to cross the Oldman River and his body was never found. His sister, Marcella, was the first white woman to come in via the Whoop-Up Trail in 1872 or 73 and she later married Joseph McFarland, a pioneer farmer of Fort Macleod. Jerry Potts, most famous of scouts, who guided the police to their destination, lived around Fort Macleod, where he died in 1896, after having faithfully served the N.W.M.P. for 22 years.

Among the many names that come to mind are Fred Kanouse, Joe Kipp, George Hauk, Fred Wachter, Ed Smith, Dick Berry and J.D. Weatherwax; Kamoose Taylor, the genial landlord of the Macleod Hotel, Kootenai Brown, first warden of Waterton Lakes Park, Jeff Davis, head bull whacker for the I.G. Baker Company, J.W. Schultz who recorded many early experiences. My father, D.W. Davis, was one of the traders who remained in Canada after the arrival of the police. He was the general manager of the I.G. Baker Company until they sold out to the Hudson's Bay Company and he was elected first M.P. for Alberta. Like J.J. Healy, he succumbed to the lure of a new frontier and went to the Yukon in 1896, where he died in 1906.

One name that appears frequently in accounts of early Alberta-Montana history is well known here, being that of Howell Harris. He first came to Alberta from Montana in 1869 and was train boss of bull trains running between Fort Benton and Fort Whoop-Up. He built Fort Conrad at the junction of the Belly and Oldman Rivers in 1871 and also built another fort near the present town of High River in 1872. He was in charge of a supply train which accompanied Governor Laird to Blackfoot Crossing where the treaty [Treaty 7] with the Indians was signed in 1877 and he was for many years a prominent rancher in southern Alberta, being the manager of the Circle Ranch north of Lethbridge which was owned by the Conrad interests. He was also a councilor of the City of Lethbridge in his later years. Another well-known Montana man who freighted on the Whoop-Up Trail was Mr. R.S. Ford, the father of Lee Ford a well-known Great Falls banker. Mr. R.S. Ford was also the first president of the Montana Stock Growers Association.

During the years the Whoop-Up Trail was the main line of commerce, the two great commercial firms with which Albertans had business were the I.G. Baker Company and T.C. Power & Brother, both of Fort Benton. The founder of the former Company was I.G. Baker and with him were associated the

Conrad brothers, W.G., C.E. and John H., who later purchased the Baker interest.

They were active in carrying on trade with Canada, particularly after the arrival of the N.W.M.P. in 1874, and they established stores at Fort Macleod, Fort Calgary and other places. T.C. Power and Brother also had stores in Fort Macleod and Fort Walsh. All these and many others whose names are now unknown, were truly the Builders of the West. Their epitaph might well be expressed in a few lines written by Sam C. Dunham, written at Circle City, Alaska in 1898—

"While others sing of the chosen few
Who o'er the fates prevail,
I will sing of the many, staunch and true,
Whose brave hearts never quail,
Who with dauntless spirit of pioneers
A state are building for coming years,
The men who blaze the trail."

During this period relations between Alberta and Montana were very free and friendly, and Fort Benton and Fort Macleod were closer neighbors than they were for many years thereafter, but the expansion of the railways in Canada and the United States brought this era to an end. In 1883 the railway reached Medicine Hat, goods came in by an all Canadian route then and the bull trains could not compete with the iron horse. Trade via the Whoop-Up Trail quickly dwindled and died. Grass grew over the deep cut ruts and in time only the experienced eye could see where the old trail had run. However, the spirit of friendship engendered in pioneer days has not vanished and with improved means of transportation and communication, the exchange of friendly visits is becoming more and more common. We have had a similar background of pioneer days, we have experienced the trials and tribulations of western agriculture, we have had many mutual interests in the past. May we have even more in the days to come.[99]

Today, 150 years after the Whoop-Up years of tensions and violent cultural clashes among and between indigenous peoples and Euro-Americans on both sides of the Medicine Line, the reserves and reservations are important, integral parts of Alberta and Montana. The

Pikuni Blackfeet elders at Old Fort Benton during the 150th anniversary of the Lame Bull Treaty. *Author's photo.*

Fort Benton levee today, long past the steamboat era, looking downstream toward Signal Point. *Photo by author.*

harsh words and rhetoric are in the past, and significant progress has been made in civil rights, yet always with more progress yet to come. Thousands of international and national tourists visit the reserves and reservations, enjoying shared cultural attractions, like Powwows, First Peoples Buffalo Jump, Head-Smashed-In Buffalo Jump and museums.

Today, memories of the Whoop-Up Trail, after 150 years, glimmer on both sides of the Medicine Line. From steamboats and bull trains to the iron horse, this first international highway from Montana to Alberta and Saskatchewan has been replaced by modern highways, in part Interstate Highway 15 from the border south and Highway 4 north. Old Fort Benton Trading Post and Fort Whoop-Up have been reconstructed, as have historic Fort Macleod and Fort Walsh, and living history brings forth the days of furs and robes and traders and Indians—and whisky, to the delight of thousands of tourists. Scores of Canadians visit Old Fort Benton and the Overholser Historical Research Center pursuing shared lives and events, family histories and academic research for books and articles. Many Montanans head north to visit Fort Whoop-Up, Fort Macleod, Galt Museum, Glenbow, Head-Smashed-In and other attractions to seek the stories and events of our shared past. We no longer drive past Captain Nels at Teton Crossing on the Whoop-Up Trail, but

A lone sentinel at Old Fort Benton. *Overholser Historical Research Center.*

202

many drive, or even walk, portions of the historic old Whoop-Up Trail, off today's main highways. Memories of the Whoop-Up Trail at 150 years, this great international avenue of trade and commerce, with its shared lifeline and culture from our past, flicker brightly at times on both sides of the Medicine Line. Here's to colorful Whoop-Up Country as we "whoop-em up" at 150 years!

NOTES

Introduction

1. The "Medicine Line" is the part of the U.S./Canadian border along the forty-ninth parallel in the West. During frontier days, when clashes between U.S. troops and indigenous peoples happened, the native tribes would cross north into British/Canadian territory for refuge after a fight. Since the land north of the forty-ninth parallel was not American territory, U.S. soldiers halted at the border, allowing the Natives to get away. This "magical" ability to stop advancing American military led Natives to term the forty-ninth parallel the "Medicine Line," a magical line of good medicine. Urban Dictionary, www.urbandictionary.com/define.php?term=Medicine%20Line.
2. While Whoop-Up Country is primarily the land of the Blackfoot, at least fourteen indigenous tribes roamed the distinctive landscape where bison once roamed, tribes whose lives depended upon that sacred animal, including the four tribes of the Blackfoot Nation, as well as the Salish, Kootenai, Pend d'Oreille, Shoshone, Bannock, Nez Perce, Gros Ventre, Crow, Assiniboine and Little Shell of Chippewa.
3. Dempsey, *Firewater*, 2.
4. Hanson, *Provisions of the Fur Trade*, 185–86.
5. Ibid., 202; Haydon, *Riders of the Plains*, 157.
6. The Old Forts Trail is an International Historic Trail that brings to life the defining moments in the opening of the Canadian and American West

through authentic experiences in this historically themed travel route. This Historic Trail connects Forts Benton and Assinniboine in Montana with Forts Walsh, Battleford and Wood Mountain Post in Saskatchewan and Forts Whoop-Up, MacLeod and Calgary in Alberta.

Chapter 1

7. Ken Robison, "Completing the Mullan Road from Mullan Pass to Fort Benton: A Harbinger of Change," in *Mullan Road*, edited by McDermott et al., 131–32.
8. Ibid.
9. Lepley, *Blackfoot Fur Trade*; Overholser, *Fort Benton*.
10. Overholser, *Fort Benton*, 355.
11. Dempsey, *Firewater*, 220–24.
12. Schultz, *My Life as an Indian*, 294.
13. Miles, *My Genealogy*, 12–14.
14. Healy, *Life and Death*, 263–64.
15. Strachan, *Blazing the Mullan Trail*, 53.
16. William Gladstone, "Views of Early Fort Benton," *Rocky Mountain Echo*, December 8, 1903.
17. Robison, *Yankees and Rebels*, 127–30.
18. *Helena Independent*, March 29, 1874.
19. Healy, *Life and Death*, 180–83.

Chapter 2

20. Wylie, *Blood on the Marias*, 155–62; Tolton, *Healy's West*, 99–101; Touchie, *Bear Child*, 106; Dempsey, *Firewater*, 46.
21. Touchie, *Bear Child*, 106.
22. Ibid., 106–7.
23. Wylie, *Blood on the Marias*, 155–58.
24. Ibid., 158–59.
25. Healy, *Life and Death*, 155.
26. Wylie, *Blood on the Marias*, 169–201. Heavy Runner was also known as Bear Chief.
27. *Helena Daily Herald*, February 9, 1870.
28. *Helena Daily Herald*, March 14, 1870.

29. *Lethbridge Herald,* July 26, 1912.

30. *Dillon Examiner*, March 8, 1922.

31. Touchie, *Bear Child*, 113–16.

32. *Great Falls Tribune,* July 2, 1935. Howell Harris recalled his second trip to Canada as the spring of 1871, yet the actual year was likely 1870—see Touchie, *Bear Child*, 110, and Kennedy and Reeves, *Inventory and Historical Description*, 9.

33. *Helena Daily Herald,* June 15, 1870.

34. Dempsey, *Firewater*, 63.

35. Kennedy and Reeves, *Inventory and Historical Description*, 92–93; Fooks, *Fort Whoop-Up*, 7–8.

36. *Helena Daily Herald*, April 8, 1873. Hugh Dempsey places this incident at an Elbow River post—see Dempsey, *Firewater*, 99.

37. *Lethbridge Herald,* July 11, 1935.

38. *Great Falls Tribune*, May 1, 1932.

Chapter 3

39. Dempsey, *Firewater*, 67–69.

40. Thomson, *Blacks in Deep Snow*; Southern Alberta Pioneers and their Descendants, www.pioneersalberta.org/profiles/s.html.

41. *Ronan Pioneer,* July 20, 1917.

42. Richard "Dick" Berry, along with brothers Isaac and James, from Calloway County, Missouri, fought with William Quantrill for the Confederacy during the Civil War. Dick and Isaac Berry rode with Quantrill during his raid on Lawrence, Kansas. See Robison, *Confederates in Montana Territory*, 90–105.

43. *Great Falls Tribune*, December 26, 1926.

44. *Great Falls Tribune,* July 2, 1935.

45. Dempsey, *Historic Sites of Alberta*; Kennedy and Reeves, *Inventory and Historical Description*.

46. Donalee Deck, "Rediscovering Farwell's Trading Post: An Interim Report on the 2010 Public Archaeology Project," *Saskatchewan Archaeological Society Newsletter* 31, no. 4 (November 2010).

47. Kennedy and Reeves, *Inventory and Historical Description*, 78.

48. Ibid., 130; *Calgary Herald*, September 15, 1967.

49. Kennedy and Reeves, *Inventory and Historical Description*, 131–32.

50. Ibid., 137–38; Dempsey, *Firewater*, 200.

Chapter 4

51. Kennedy and Reeves, *Inventory and Historical Description*, 29–31; Schultz, *Wolfers*.

52. Dempsey, *Firewater*, 167; Kennedy and Reeves, *Inventory and Historical Description*, 29–30.

53. Dempsey, *Firewater*, 167.

54. *Great Falls Tribune*, April 6, 1930.

55. *Helena Weekly Herald*, April 23, 1874.

56. *Calgary Herald*, January 26, 1907.

57. *Helena Independent*, November 17, 1886. The Salteaux are a First Nations Ojibwa Chippewa people, although John Duval is wrong, for the tribe was North Assiniboine.

58. *Helena Herald*, April 17, 1874.

Chapter 5

59. *Canadian Illustrated News 1874–1875*. The Great March West was covered by traveling artist and journalist Henri Julien in *Canadian Illustrated News*, "Six Months in the Wilds of the North-West." His reports are available online at www.canadiana.ca/view/oocihm.8_06230.

60. *Canadian Illustrated News*, February 13, 1875, 99.

61. Members of the Mounted Police wrote accounts of the march, including Cecil Denny, *Calgary Herald*, September 7, 1904; See also Denny, *Denny's Trek*, 2004.

62. Overholser, *Fort Benton*, 360.

63. *Calgary Herald*, September 7, 1904.

64. *Calgary Herald*, September 13, 1904; Dempsey, *Firewater*, 213.

65. McDougall, *On Western Trails*, 66–67.

66. Sharp, *Whoop-Up Country*, 93.

67. *Benton Weekly Record*, February 15, 1875. This newspaper began publication in early 1875, the first newspaper in northern Montana Territory.

68. Sharp, *Whoop-Up Country*, 92–95; *Benton Weekly Record*, March 5, 1880.

69. *Fort Benton River Press*, April 8, 1885.

Chapter 6

70. *Dillon Examiner*, August 18, 1926.

71. *Helena Weekly Herald*, July 15, 1875.

72. *Helena Weekly Herald*, July 29, 1875.

73. *Helena Independent*, July 25, 1875.

74. *Benton Weekly Record*, July 31, 1875.

75. *Benton Weekly Record*, August 7, 1875.

76. *Benton Weekly Record*, February 15, 1878.

77. *Benton Weekly Record*, August 14, 21, 1875.

78. *Benton Weekly Record*, September 11, 1875.

79. *Helena Weekly Herald*, October 7, 1875.

80. *Benton Weekly Record*, October 9, 1875.

81. *Benton Weekly Record*, November 6, 1875.

82. *Winnipeg, Manitoba Free Press, Canada*, June 23, 1876.

83. *Winnipeg, Manitoba Free Press, Canada*, March 16, 1882; *Benton Weekly Record*, April 6, 1882.

84. *Fort Benton River Press*, May 19, 1886.

Chapter 7

85. *Benton Record Weekly*, January 16, 1880.

86. Kennedy and Reeves, *Inventory and Historical Description*, 42–43; *Helena Weekly Herald*, October 7, December 2, 1875.

87. *Helena Weekly Herald*, October 28, 1875.

88. Kim Briggeman, "A Frontier Survivor," *Missoula Magazine*, Winter 2011–12.

89. Montana Historical Society Small Collection 1234 1/1, Reminiscences of Charles Schafft, Letter to John Armstrong, April 24, 1887.

90. *Benton Weekly Record*, January 16, 1880.

91. Reminiscences of Charles Schafft.

92. See *New North-west*, November 28, December 12, 1884.

93. *Mineral Independent*, July 29, 1926. For more about James W. Brown's life and Civil War experiences see Robison, *Montana Territory and the Civil War*, 59–64.

94. Conrad High School, *The Whoop-Up Trail 1922*, annual yearbook.

95. Ibid.

96. *Conrad Independent*, April 20, 1939.

97. *Fort Benton River Press*, July 8, 1954.
98. *Fort Benton River Press*, July 8, 1954.
99. *Fort Benton River Press*, July 28, 1954.

BIBLIOGRAPHY

Newspapers/Journals

Note: These are Montana periodicals unless otherwise noted.

Benton Weekly Record
Calgary Herald (Canada)
Canadian Illustrated News (Canada)
Conrad Independent
Dillon Examiner
Fort Benton River Press
Great Falls Tribune
Helena Daily Herald
Helena Independent
Helena Weekly Herald
Lethbridge Herald (Canada)
Manitoba Free Press (Winnipeg, Canada)
Mineral Independent (Superior)
Missoula Magazine
New North-west (Deer Lodge)
Rocky Mountain Echo
Ronan Pioneer
Saskatchewan Archaeological Society Newsletter

Other Sources

Anderson, Frank W. *Fort Walsh and the Cypress Hills*. Humboldt, SK: Gopher Books, 1999.

Arthur, Jim, ed. *Retracing Kipp Family Trails: A Collection of Stories and Pictures of the Kipp Family and the Country They Lived In, with Stories by Octavia Kipp*. Lewistown: Central Montana, 1997.

Baker, William M., ed. *The Mounted Police and Prairie Society, 1873–1919*. Regina, SK: Canadian Plains Research Center, University of Regina, 1998.

Berry, Gerald L. *The Whoop-Up Trail: Alberta–Montana Relationships*. Edmonton, AB: Applied Art Products Ltd., 1953.

———. *The Whoop-Up Trail: Early Days in Alberta—Montana*. Occasional Paper No. 29. Lethbridge, AB: Lethbridge Historical Society, 1995.

Blackfeet Heritage Program. *Blackfeet Heritage, 1907–1908*. Browning, MT: Blackfeet Heritage Program, 1980.

Briggeman, Kim. "A Frontier Survivor." *Missoula Magazine*, Winter 2011–12.

Dempsey, Hugh A. *The Amazing Death of Calf Shirt and Other Blackfoot Stories: Three Hundred Years of Blackfoot History*. Norman: University of Oklahoma Press, 1994.

———. *A Blackfoot Winter Count*. Occasional Paper No. 1. Calgary: Glenbow Foundation, 1965.

———. *Crowfoot: Chief of the Blackfoot*. Norman: University of Oklahoma Press, 1972.

———. *Firewater: The Impact of the Whisky Trade on the Blackfoot Nation*. Calgary: Fifth House, 2002.

———. *Historic Sites of Alberta*. Edmonton: Alberta Government Travel Bureau, Department of Industry and Development, 1966.

———. *Jerry Potts, Plainsman*. Occasional Paper No. 3. Calgary: Glenbow Foundation, 1966.

———. *Red Crow: Warrior Chief*. Saskatoon, SK: Western Producer Prairie Books, 1980.

———. *The Vengeful Wife and Other Blackfoot Stories*. Norman: University of Oklahoma Press, 2003.

Denny, Sir Cecil. *Denny's Trek: A Mountie's Memoir of the March West*. Surrey, BC: Heritage House Publishing Company, 2004.

Ege, Robert J. *Tell Baker to Strike Them Hard*. Bellevue, NE: Old Army Press, 1970.

Fooks, Georgia Green. *Fort Whoop-Up: Alberta's First and Most Notorious Whisky Fort*. Occasional Paper No. 11. Lethbridge, AB: Whoop-Up Country Chapter. Historical Society of Alberta, 1983.

The Frontier Art of R.B. Nevitt: Surgeon, North-West Mounted Police, 1874–78. Calgary: Glenbow-Alberta Institute, n.d.

Hanson, James A. *Provisions of the Fur Trade*, vol. 6. *The Encyclopedia of Trade Goods.* Chadron, NE: Museum of the Fur Trade, 2017.

———. *When Skins Were Money: A History of the Fur Trade.* Chadron, NE: Museum of the Fur Trade, 2005.

Haydon, A. *The Riders of the Plains.* Rutland, VT: Charles E. Tuttle Company, 1971.

Healy, John J. *Life and Death on the Upper Missouri: The Frontier Sketches of Johnny Healy.* Edited by Ken Robison. N.p., Create Space Independent Publishing Platform, 2013.

Hildebrandt, Walter, and Brian Hubner. *The Cypress Hills: The Land and Its People.* Saskatoon, SK: Purich Publishing, 1994.

Hungry Wolf, Adolf. *The Blackfeet Papers*, vol. 1. *Pikunni History and Culture.* Skookumchuck, BC: Good Medicine Cultural Foundation, 2006.

Kennedy, Margaret A. *The Whiskey Trade of the Northwestern Plains: A Multidisciplinary Study.* New York: Peter Lang Publishing, 1997.

Kennedy, M.A., and B.O.K. Reeves. *An Inventory and Historical Description of Whiskey Posts in Southern Alberta.* Edmonton: Historic Sites Service, Old St. Stephen's College, 1984.

Lepley, John G. *Birthplace of Montana: A History of Fort Benton.* Missoula, MT: Pictorial Histories Publishing, 1999.

———. *Blackfoot Fur Trade on the Upper Missouri.* Missoula, MT: Pictorial Histories Publishing, 2004.

———. *The Madame and the Four Johns: Fort Benton's Lawless Years of Gold.* Fort Benton, MT: River & Plains Society, 2013.

———. *Packets to Paradise: Steamboating to Fort Benton.* Missoula, MT: Pictorial Histories Publishing, 2001.

Long, Philip S. *Jerry Potts: Scout, Frontiersman and Hero.* Calgary: Bonanza Books, 1974.

Lowell, James Howard. *An Antietam Veteran's Montana Journey: The Lost Memoir of James Howard Lowell.* Edited by Katherine Seaton Squires. Charleston, SC: The History Press, 2018

McBride, Sister Genevieve, OSV. *The Bird Tail.* New York: Vantage Press, 1974.

McDermott, Paul D., et al, eds. *The Mullan Road: Carving a Passage through the Frontier Northwest, 1859–62.* Missoula, MT: Mountain Press Publishing, 2015.

McDougall, John. *On Western Trails in the Early Seventies Frontier Pioneer Life in The Canadian North-West.* Toronto: William Briggs, 1911.

Miles, Walter K. *My Genealogy*. Vol. 2. N.p., privately printed, n.d.

Murphy, James E. *Half Interest in a Silver Dollar: The Saga of Charles E. Conrad*. Missoula, MT: Mountain Press Publishing Company, 1983.

Nevitt, R.B. *Winter at Fort Macleod*. Edited by Hugh A. Dempsey. Calgary: Glenbow-Alberta Institute, McClelland and Stewart West, 1974.

Overholser, Joel. *Fort Benton: World's Innermost Port*. Helena, MT: Falcon Press, 1987.

Robison, Ken. *Confederates in Montana Territory: In the Shadow of Price's Army*. Charleston, SC: The History Press, 2014.

———. *Montana Territory and the Civil War: A Frontier Forged on the Battlefield*. Charleston, SC: The History Press, 2013.

———. *Yankees and Rebels on the Upper Missouri: Steamboats, Gold and Peace*. Charleston, SC: The History Press, 2016.

Royal Canadian Mounted Police, comp. *Opening Up the West: 1874–1881*. Toronto: Coles, 1973.

Schultz, James Willard. *Friends of My Life as an Indian*. Boston: Houghton Mifflin Company, 1923.

———. *My Life as an Indian*. Boston: Houghton, Mifflin Company, 1907.

———. *The Wolfers*. Fort Benton, MT: River and Plains Society, 2007.

Sharp, Paul F. *Whoop-Up Country: The Canadian West, 1865–1885*. Minneapolis: University of Minnesota Press, 1955.

Strachan, John. *Blazing the Mullan Trail: Connecting the Headwaters of the Missouri and Columbia Rivers*. New York: Edward Eberstadt & Sons, 1952.

Thomson, Colin A. *Blacks in Deep Snow: Black Pioneers in Canada*. Ontario: J.M. Dent & Sons, 1979.

Tolton, Gordon E. *Healy's West: The Life and Times of John J. Healy*. Calgary: Heritage House Publishing, 2014.

Tolton, Gordon E., et al., eds. *The Last Blast: The Fur Trade in Whoop-Up Country*. Lethbridge, AB: Fort Whoop-Up Interpretive Society, 2013.

Touchie, Rodger D. *Bear Child: The Life and Times of Jerry Potts*. Surrey, AB: Heritage House Publishing Company, 2005.

Wissler, Clark, and Alice Beck Kehoe. *Amshkapi Pikuni The Blackfoot People*. Albany: State University of New York Press, 2012.

Wylie, Paul R. *Blood on the Marias: The Baker Massacre*. Norman: University of Oklahoma Press, 2016.

INDEX

ABOUT THE AUTHOR

K en Robison is a chronicler of neglected western history who lives in Great Falls, Montana. Ken, a Montana native, is historian at the Overholser Historical Research Center in Fort Benton, Sun River Valley Historical Society, Great Falls/Cascade County Historic Preservation Commission and Big Sky Country National Heritage Area. Ken is a retired U.S. Navy captain after a career in naval intelligence. The Montana Historical Society has honored Ken as a Montana Heritage Keeper. His books include: *Montanans in the Great War: Open Warfare Over There*, *World War I Montana: The Treasure State Prepares*, *Montana Territory and the Civil War: A Frontier Forged on the Battlefield*, *Confederates in Montana Territory: In the Shadow of Price's Army* and *Yankees and Rebels on the Upper Missouri: Steamboats, Gold and Peace*. He is coauthor of *Black Americans in the Civil Rights Movement in the West*, *Montana, A Cultural Medley: Stories of Our Ethnic Diversity*, *Beyond Schoolmarms and Madams: Montana Women's Stories* and *The Mullan Road: Carving a Passage through the Frontier Northwest, 1859 to 1862*. Ken edited *Life and Death on the Upper Missouri: The Frontier Sketches of Johnny Healy*. Visit Ken Robison History at https://www.kenrobisonhistory.com.